★ ★ ★ ★ ★ ★ ★ ★ ★ ★ ★ ★ ★ ★ ★ ★ ★ ★

THE UNITED STATES
CONSTITUTION

what it **says**,
what it **means**

★ ★ ★ ★ ★ ★ ★ ★ ★ ★ ★ ★ ★ ★ ★ ★ ★ ★

The text of the United States Constitution,
including an understandable description of each
Article and Amendment, right in the palm of your hand.

A HIP POCKET GUIDE

OXFORD
UNIVERSITY PRESS

Oxford   New York
Auckland Bangkok Buenos Aires Cape Town Chennai
Dar es Salaam Delhi Hong Kong Istanbul Karachi Kolkata
Kuala Lumpur Madrid Melbourne Mexico City Mumbai
Nairobi São Paulo Shanghai Taipei Tokyo Toronto

Published by Oxford University Press, Inc.
198 Madison Avenue, New York, New York, 10016
http://www.oup.com/us

Academic Advisor: Don Ritchie

www.JusticeLearning.org

Library of Congress Cataloging-in-Publication Data

United States.
[Constitution]
The United States Constitution : what it says, what it means :
a hip pocket guide / by The Founding Fathers and JusticeLearning.org.
p. cm.
ISBN-13 978-0-19-530443-5

1. United States. Constitution. 2. Constitutions—United States.
3. Law—United States—Interpretation and construction.
I. JusticeLearning.org. II. Title.
KF4527.U548 2005
342.7302--dc22
2005012362

14 15 16 17 18 19 20

Printed in China

Introduction

By Caroline Kennedy

By day, they are displayed in a majestic rotunda in the National Archives, but at night they are lowered into a vault strong enough to withstand a nuclear attack. They are the four pages of the original U.S. Constitution, drafted in 1787, the framework for all that our nation is now and all that it has yet to become.

The Constitution sets forth the structure of our federal government—which is divided into three branches with the familiar system of checks and balances—and allocates power between the federal government and the states. It provides protection against the abuse of power and for the rights of minorities so that Americans would never again be subjected to tyranny. Together with the Bill of Rights, added in 1791, it provides the most comprehensive protection for individual rights and liberties in the world.

Today we are at war overseas, in Iraq and in Afghanistan, while at home Americans are struggling with competing visions of who we are and who we should be. These struggles are rooted in the values of freedom and democracy on which this country was founded. A new generation is trying to meet its obligation to define America's future in an age of globalization while still holding our nation true to our shared ideals. This ideological struggle will be played out in foreign and domestic policy debates in Washington, D.C., and in statehouses and courtrooms across this country. But it will also be played out in debates at family dinner tables, in our schools and our churches, in our hospitals, our national parks, on college campuses, and in the workplace.

The stakes could not be higher. The resolution of these debates, and their impact on our society is unknown, but we can be sure that they will be decided by ordinary Americans, because when the Founding Fathers drafted the U.S.

Constitution, they placed ultimate sovereignty in us with the immortal words, "We The People, in order to form a more perfect Union . . . do ordain and establish . . . the Constitution of the United States."

But the document is only the starting point. As Alexander Hamilton wrote, "The sacred rights of mankind are not to be rummaged for among old parchments or musty records. They are written, as with a sunbeam, in the whole volume of human nature, by the hand of the divinity itself. . . ." Unlike almost any other country, America was founded on ideas and values—freedom, equality, tolerance and diversity. The fact that ours is the oldest written constitution still in use is a testament to the enduring power of those ideas, and to the skill with which the founders framed them. It is easy to take this heritage for granted, but these ideals have survived only because individual citizens in war and in peace time have sacrificed and struggled to breathe life into the words of the sacred text and to define those words anew for each generation.

It is important to remember that our Constitution, for all its virtues, was and is not perfect. Many early patriots, including Thomas Jefferson and Thomas Paine, believed it betrayed the spirit of liberty that was at the heart of the American Revolution. They opposed a strong central government, fearing it would bring a return to tyranny. Others objected that it did not contain enough protection for individual rights. The original Constitution also failed to resolve the issue of slavery even though in 1790 there were seven hundred thousand slaves out of a population of almost four million. This failure dominated nineteenth-century politics and culminated in the Civil War. Six hundred thousand Americans died during that conflict, which remains the bloodiest war in American history.

Only after the war ended was the Constitution amended to abolish slavery and guarantee voting rights, due process, and equal protection of the laws. It took another fifty years before a constitutional amendment allowed women to vote, and a century before the civil rights movement forced the

United States to begin fulfilling the promises of the Declaration of Independence to African Americans. Led by parents who believed so strongly in the cause that they were willing to put their children in danger, and by children who by the power of their example showed the way to a more just America, the civil rights movement and the movements that followed demonstrated the power of individual citizens to transform our society through a commitment to the rule of law. That commitment was anchored in the U.S. Constitution.

Now it is our turn. We can only contribute if we are informed and engaged, if we understand our history and our rights. Harry Truman once said that in a democracy, the highest office is that of citizen, and the Constitution places the nation's future in our hands.

Today, our society is grappling with fundamental questions that will shape our lives for years to come. The government has expanded its ability to monitor, interrogate, search, and detain American citizens, but how much of our individual freedoms are we Americans willing to give up in order to increase public safety? And in the most private areas of our lives the balance of power may also be shifting, as we struggle to reach a national consensus on issues surrounding the beginning and the end of life. Under what circumstances can a woman legally terminate a pregnancy? What is the role of government in patient and family decisions to refuse medical treatment that would prolong life?

The principles embedded in our Constitution will determine the answers to these questions and others that affect our lives in more ordinary ways: When can students be subjected to random drug testing? Strip searches? Is file-sharing protected by our right to freedom of speech? What kinds of admissions policies used by academic institutions seeking to create intellectually diverse communities are unconstitutional? In a civilized society, under what circumstances is the death penalty considered cruel and unusual punishment? What is the proper role for religion in our schools, our courtrooms?

When I was writing a book on the Bill of Rights I met people from across this country: Native Americans fighting to preserve their sacred land from encroaching development, Ku Klux Klan members seeking to exercise their freedom of speech, death-row inmates fighting for a fair trial, civil rights leaders seeking justice for historically disenfranchised Americans. Most of these people never thought that they would have to fight for their rights, but when those rights were threatened, each of them realized that their commitment to America required them to step forward and fight so that those rights would be preserved for the rest of us.

A woman who successfully sued the government to prevent the kind of unconstitutional intimidation and harassment that the FBI engaged in during the civil rights and anti-war movements, put it best: "It is up to each of us to create a government that is close to our heart's desire," she said, adding ominously, "because, if you don't do it, somebody else will."

The future of the United States is too important to leave it to someone else. Each of us must take the time and make the effort to become informed about our history, our government, and our rights. At times, history can seem disconnected from present-day reality, but understanding how laws have been used to bring about change in the past provides us with the tools to change the future. We must study history to make history and this pocket Constitution is a great place to start.

Oliver Wendell Holmes, Jr., the great Justice of the Supreme Court, wrote of the Constitution, "It is an experiment, as all life is an experiment." The outcome is unknown and ongoing, but the success of a life, like that of the Constitution, depends on our willingness to give of ourselves.

THE CONSTITUTION OF THE UNITED STATES OF AMERICA

Preamble

We the People of the United States, in Order to form a more perfect Union, establish Justice, insure domestic Tranquility, provide for the common defence, promote the general Welfare, and secure the Blessings of Liberty to ourselves and our Posterity, do ordain and establish this Constitution for the United States of America.

What it means

The preamble is the introduction to the Constitution. It outlines the general goals of the framers: to create a just government, insure peace, an adequate national defense, and a healthy, free nation. With its first three words, "We the People," the preamble emphasizes that the nation is to be ruled by the people—not a king or dictator, not the president, Supreme Court Justices, members of Congress or state legislators. Importantly, the Supreme Court held in 1905 (in *Jacobson* v. *Massachusetts*) that the preamble is not a source of federal power or individuals rights. Rather all rights and powers are set out in the articles and amendments that follow.

Article I, Section 1

All legislative Powers herein granted shall be vested in a Congress of the United States, which shall consist of a Senate and House of Representatives.

What it means

The framers of the Constitution separated the powers of government into three branches, granting legislative power (the power to pass laws) to Congress, executive power (the power to administer the laws) to the president, and judicial power (the power to interpret and enforce the laws) to the courts. The unique and limited powers of Congress are contained in Article I.

The framers believed that this separation of powers would ensure that no one person or group of persons would be able to create, administer, and enforce the laws at the same time and that each branch would be a check on the power of the other two branches. Under this scheme, Congress cannot give its own lawmaking powers to the executive or judicial branch. The courts are charged with ensuring that the three branches act independently and do not overreach their delegated powers. But in some instances, two branches of government are required to work together. For example, the Senate must approve the president's appointments to the Supreme Court, and the president has the power to veto acts of Congress or to pardon convicted criminals.

Another important principle is contained in Article I, Section 1: the federal government's power is limited to what is written in the Constitution. These are known as "enumerated powers." If the Constitution does not specifically give a power to the federal government, the power is left to the states.

Article I, Section 1 also requires that Congress be bicameral, that is, it should be divided into two houses, the Senate and the House of Representatives. At the time the Constitution was adopted, several of the states and the Continental Congress had only one lawmaking body. The creation of two legislative bodies reflected a compromise between the power of the states and the power of the people. The number of seats in the House of Representatives is based on population. The larger and more urban states have more representatives than the more rural, less-populated states. But the Senate gives power to the states equally, with two senators from each state. In order to create a law, any proposed legislation must be passed by both the House of Representatives and the Senate and be approved (or at least not vetoed) by the president.

Article I, Section 2

The House of Representatives shall be composed of Members chosen every second Year by the People of the several States, and the Electors in each State shall have the Qualifications requisite for Electors of the most numerous Branch of the State Legislature.

No Person shall be a Representative who shall not have attained to the Age of twenty five Years, and been seven Years a Citizen of the United States, and who shall not, when elected, be an Inhabitant of that State in which he shall be chosen.

[Representatives and direct Taxes shall be apportioned among the several States which may be included within this Union, according to their respective Numbers, which shall be determined by adding to the whole Number of free Persons, including those bound to Service for a Term of Years, and excluding Indians not taxed, three fifths of all other Persons.][1] The actual Enumeration shall be made within three Years after the first Meeting of the Congress of the United States, and within every subsequent Term of ten Years, in such Manner as they shall by Law direct. The Number of Representatives shall not exceed one for every thirty Thousand, but each State shall have at Least one Representative; and until such enumeration shall be made, the State of New Hampshire shall be entitled to chuse three, Massachusetts eight, Rhode-Island and Providence Plantations one, Connecticut five, New-York six, New Jersey four, Pennsylvania eight, Delaware one, Maryland six, Virginia ten, North Carolina five, South Carolina five, and Georgia three.

When vacancies happen in the Representation from any State, the Executive Authority thereof shall issue Writs of Election to fill such Vacancies.

The House of Representatives shall chuse their Speaker and other Officers; and shall have the sole Power of Impeachment.

---

1. Modified by Amendment XIV, Section 2.

What it means

Article I, Section 2 specifies that the House of Representatives be composed of members who are chosen every two years by the people of the states. There are only three qualifications: a representative must be at least twenty-five years old, must have been a citizen of the United States for at least seven years, and must live in the state from which he or she is chosen. Efforts by both Congress and the states to add requirements for office, such as durational residency requirements or loyalty oaths, have been rejected by Congress and the courts.

In 1966, the Supreme Court used the language, "chosen. . . by the people of the several States" in Article I, Section 2, to recognize a federal right to vote in congressional elections. This right along with the equal protection clause of Amendment XIV, was later used by the Supreme Court to require that each congressional district contain roughly the same number of people, ensuring that one person's vote in a congressional election be worth as much as another's.

Article I, Section 2 also creates the way in which congressional districts are to be divided among the states. A difficult and critical sticking point at the Constitutional Convention was how to count a state's population, particularly whether slaves would be counted for purposes of both representation and taxation. If slaves were considered property, they would not be counted at all; if they were considered persons, they would be counted fully—just as women, children, and others who could not vote were counted. Ironically, Southern slave-owners, who considered slaves their property, wanted slaves to be fully counted in order to increase their own political power in Congress. After extended debate, the framers agreed to the three-fifths compromise—three-fifths of the total number of slaves would be included in a state's population total (note that the framers never use the word slaves in the document). Following the Civil War, the formula was changed with the passage of Amendment XIII, which abolished slavery, and Amendment XIV, Section 2, which specifically repealed the three-fifths rule.

This section also establishes the census (enumeration): every ten years, every adult in the country must answer a survey—a monumental task when people move as often as they do and when some people have no homes at all. Based on these surveys, Congress must determine how many representatives (at least one required) are to come from each state and how federal resources are to be distributed among the states. The Constitution itself set the number of House members from each of the original thirteen states that was used until the completion of the first census.

In 1929 Congress limited the House of Representatives to 435 members and established a formula to determine how many districts would be in each state. For example, following the 2000 census, southern and western states like Texas, Florida and California gained population and thus added representatives, while northern states like Pennsylvania lost several members.

Congress left it to state legislatures to draw district lines. As a result, at the time of a census, the political party in power in each state legislature is able to define new districts that favor its own candidates, affecting who can win elections for the House of Representatives in the following decade. This process—redrawing district lines to favor a particular party— is often referred to as gerrymandering.

Article I, Section 2 also specifies other operating rules for the House of Representatives. When a member of the House dies or resigns during the term, the governor of that state can call for a special election to fill the vacancy. The House of Representatives chooses its own Speaker of the House, who is in line to become the president, if both the president and vice president are unable to serve.

Lastly, this section specifies that only the House of Representatives holds the power of impeachment. Members of the House can charge a president, vice president, or any civil officer of the United States with "Treason, Bribery or other high Crimes and Misdemeanors" (see Article II, Section 4). A trial on the charges is then held in the Senate.

This happened during the term of President Clinton. The House of Representatives investigated the president and brought charges against him. Members of the House acted as prosecutors during an impeachment trial in the Senate (see Article 1, Section 3). President Clinton was not convicted of the charges and he completed his second term as president.

Article I, Section 3

The Senate of the United States shall be composed of two Senators from each State, [chosen by the Legislature thereof,]² for six Years; and each Senator shall have one Vote.

Immediately after they shall be assembled in Consequence of the first Election, they shall be divided as equally as may be into three Classes. The Seats of the Senators of the first Class shall be vacated at the Expiration of the second Year, of the second Class at the Expiration of the fourth Year, and of the third Class at the Expiration of the sixth Year, so that one third may be chosen every second Year; [and if Vacancies happen by Resignation, or otherwise, during the Recess of the Legislature of any State, the Executive thereof may make temporary Appointments until the next Meeting of the Legislature, which shall then fill such Vacancies.]³

No Person shall be a Senator who shall not have attained to the Age of thirty Years, and been nine Years a Citizen of the United States, and who shall not, when elected, be an Inhabitant of that State for which he shall be chosen.

The Vice President of the United States shall be President of the Senate, but shall have no Vote, unless they be equally divided.

The Senate shall chuse their other Officers, and also a President pro tempore, in the Absence of the Vice President, or when he shall exercise the Office of President of the United States.

2. Modified by Amendment XVII.
3. Modified by Amendment XVII.

The Senate shall have the sole Power to try all Impeachments. When sitting for that Purpose, they shall be on Oath or Affirmation. When the President of the United States is tried, the Chief Justice shall preside: And no Person shall be convicted without the Concurrence of two thirds of the Members present.

Judgment in Cases of Impeachment shall not extend further than to removal from Office, and disqualification to hold and enjoy any Office of honor, Trust or Profit under the United States: but the Party convicted shall nevertheless be liable and subject to Indictment, Trial, Judgment and Punishment, according to Law.

What it means

The Senate, which now has one hundred members, has two senators from each state. Until 1913, senators were elected by their state legislatures. But with the adoption of Amendment XVII, senators have been elected directly by the people of each state. There are several exclusive requirements to be a senator: he or she must be over thirty years of age, must have been an American citizen for at least nine years, and must live in the state he or she represents. Senators can serve for an unlimited number of six-year terms. Senatorial elections are held on a staggered basis so that one-third of the Senate is elected every two years. If a senator leaves office before the end of his or her term, Amendment XVII now provides that the governor of his or her state sets the time for a new election. The state legislature may authorize the governor to temporarily fill the vacant seat.

The vice president of the United States is also the president of the Senate. He or she normally has no vote but can act as a tiebreaker if the Senate is equally divided on a proposed bill or nomination. The Senate also chooses officers to lead them through their work. One of the officers, the president pro tempore ("president for a time"), presides over the Senate when the vice president is not available and, like the

Speaker of the House, is in the line of succession should the president or the vice president be unable to serve.

While the House of Representatives has the job of bringing charges of impeachment to remove a president, vice president, or other civil officer, such as a federal judge, it is the Senate that is responsible for conducting the trial and deciding whether the individual is to be removed from office. The Chief Justice of the Supreme Court presides over an impeachment trial of the president. The members of the Senate act as the jury and the vote of two-thirds of those Senators present is necessary to remove an official from office. Once an official is removed, he or she may still be prosecuted criminally or sued, just like any other citizen.

Article I, Section 4

The Times, Places and Manner of holding Elections for Senators and Representatives, shall be prescribed in each State by the Legislature thereof; but the Congress may at any time by Law make or alter such Regulations, except as to the Places of chusing Senators.

The Congress shall assemble at least once in every Year, and such Meeting shall be [on the first Monday in December,][4] unless they shall by Law appoint a different Day.

What it means

Article I, Section 4 gives state legislatures the task of determining how congressional elections are held. For example, the state legislature determines when an election is scheduled, how voters can register, and where they can cast their ballots.

Congress has the right to change the state rules and provide national protections for the right to vote. The first federal election law, which among other things prohibited false registration, bribery, and making false returns, passed

4. Modified by Amendment XX, Section 2.

after the Civil War as a means of enforcing the prohibition against racial discrimination in voting contained in Amendment XV. With the passage of the Civil Rights Acts of 1957 and 1964 and the Voting Rights Act of 1965, Congress enacted greater protections for the right to vote in federal, state, and local elections.

As a general rule Congress sets its own schedule for how frequently it meets. The Constitution provides only that it must meet at least once a year. Amendment XX, Section 2 now provides that the first meeting of Congress begin at noon on January 3 of each year, unless the members specify a different schedule.

Article I, Section 5

Each House shall be the Judge of the Elections, Returns and Qualifications of its own Members, and a Majority of each shall constitute a Quorum to do Business; but a smaller Number may adjourn from day to day, and may be authorized to compel the Attendance of absent Members, in such Manner, and under such Penalties as each House may provide.

Each House may determine the Rules of its Proceedings, punish its Members for disorderly Behaviour, and, with the Concurrence of two thirds, expel a Member.

Each House shall keep a Journal of its Proceedings, and from time to time publish the same, excepting such Parts as may in their Judgment require Secrecy; and the Yeas and Nays of the Members of either House on any question shall, at the Desire of one fifth of those Present, be entered on the Journal.

Neither House, during the Session of Congress, shall, without the Consent of the other, adjourn for more than three days, nor to any other Place than that in which the two Houses shall be sitting.

What it means

The House of Representatives and the Senate are each in charge of deciding whether an election of one of its own members is legitimate. Like a judge, Congress has the power to hear witnesses to help them decide. Similarly, the House and Senate can establish their own rules, punish members for disorderly behavior and, if two-thirds agree, expel a member.

Both the House and Senate need a quorum to do business —this means that a majority of its members must be present. A full majority of members need not vote, but must be present and capable of voting. Both bodies must keep and publish a journal of their proceedings, including how members voted. Congress can decide that some discussions and votes are to be kept secret, but if one fifth of the members demand that a vote be recorded, it must be. Neither the House nor the Senate can close down or move proceedings from their usual location for a period longer than three days without the consent of the other chamber.

Article I, Section 6

The Senators and Representatives shall receive a Compensation for their Services, to be ascertained by Law, and paid out of the Treasury of the United States. They shall in all Cases, except Treason, Felony and Breach of the Peace, be privileged from Arrest during their Attendance at the Session of their respective Houses, and in going to and returning from the same; and for any Speech or Debate in either House, they shall not be questioned in any other Place.

No Senator or Representative shall, during the Time for which he was elected, be appointed to any civil Office under the Authority of the United States, which shall have been created, or the Emoluments whereof shall have been encreased during such time; and no Person holding any Office under the United States, shall be a Member of either House during his Continuance in Office.

What it means

Members of Congress are to be paid for their work from the U.S. Treasury. Amendment XXVII prohibits members from raising their own salaries in the current session, so congressional votes on pay increases do not take effect until the next session of Congress.

Article I, Section 6 also protects legislators from arrests in civil lawsuits while they are in session but they may be arrested in criminal matters. To prevent prosecutors and others from using the courts to intimidate a legislator because they do not like their views, legislators are granted immunity from criminal prosecution and civil lawsuit for the things they say and the work they do as legislators.

To ensure the separation of powers between the legislative, judicial and executive branches of government, Article I, Section 6 prohibits a senator or representative from holding any other federal office during his or her service in Congress.

Article I, Section 7

All Bills for raising Revenue shall originate in the House of Representatives; but the Senate may propose or concur with Amendments as on other Bills.

Every Bill which shall have passed the House of Representatives and the Senate, shall, before it become a Law, be presented to the President of the United States; If he approve he shall sign it, but if not he shall return it, with his Objections to that House in which it shall have originated, who shall enter the Objections at large on their Journal, and proceed to reconsider it. If after such Reconsideration two thirds of that House shall agree to pass the Bill, it shall be sent, together with the Objections, to the other House, by which it shall likewise be reconsidered, and if approved by two thirds of that House, it shall become a Law. But in all such Cases the Votes of both Houses shall be determined by Yeas and Nays, and the Names of the Persons voting for and against the Bill shall be entered on the Journal of each

House respectively. If any Bill shall not be returned by the President within ten Days (Sundays excepted) after it shall have been presented to him, the Same shall be a Law, in like Manner as if he had signed it, unless the Congress by their Adjournment prevent its Return, in which Case it shall not be a Law.

Every Order, Resolution, or Vote to which the Concurrence of the Senate and House of Representatives may be necessary (except on a question of Adjournment) shall be presented to the President of the United States; and before the Same shall take Effect, shall be approved by him, or being disapproved by him, shall be repassed by two thirds of the Senate and House of Representatives, according to the Rules and Limitations prescribed in the Case of a Bill.

What it means

The House of Representatives must begin the process when it comes to raising and spending money. It is the chamber where all taxing and spending bills start. The Senate can offer changes and must ultimately approve the bills before they go to the president, but only the House can introduce a bill that involves taxes.

When proposed laws are approved by both the House and Senate, they go to the president. If the president signs the bill, it becomes law at the time of the signature, unless the bill provides for a different start date. If the president does nothing for ten days, not including Sundays, the bill automatically becomes law, except in the last ten days of the legislative term. In that time, the president can use a "pocket veto"—by doing nothing, the legislation is automatically vetoed.

If the president does not like the legislation, he or she can veto the bill, list objections, and send it back for reconsideration to the chamber where it originated. If the president vetoes a bill, the bill must be passed again with the votes of two-thirds of the House and the Senate for it to become law. Congress also can change the bill to make it more acceptable to the president. Although for political reasons presidents are cautious about vetoing legislation, the threat of a veto will often press members of Congress to work out a compromise. Similarly, if Congress has the ability to override a veto, it is likely the president will make every effort to compromise on the issue.

Article I, Section 8

The Congress shall have Power To lay and collect Taxes, Duties, Imposts and Excises, to pay the Debts and provide for the common Defence and general Welfare of the United States; but all Duties, Imposts and Excises shall be uniform throughout the United States;

To borrow Money on the credit of the United States;

To regulate Commerce with foreign Nations, and among the several states, and with the Indian Tribes;

To establish an uniform Rule of Naturalization, and uniform Laws on the subject of Bankruptcies throughout the United States;

To coin Money, regulate the Value thereof, and of foreign Coin, and fix the Standard of Weights and Measures;

To provide for the Punishment of counterfeiting the Securities and current Coin of the United States;

To establish Post Offices and post Roads;

To promote the Progress of Science and useful Arts, by securing for limited Times to Authors and Inventors the exclusive Right to their respective Writings and Discoveries;

To constitute Tribunals inferior to the supreme Court;

To define and punish Piracies and Felonies committed on the high Seas, and Offences against the Law of Nations;

To declare War, grant Letters of Marque and Reprisal, and make Rules concerning Captures on Land and Water;

To raise and support Armies, but no Appropriation of Money to that Use shall be for a longer Term than two Years;

To provide and maintain a Navy;

To make Rules for the Government and Regulation of the land and naval Forces;

To provide for calling forth the Militia to execute the Laws of the Union, suppress Insurrections and repel Invasions;

To provide for organizing, arming, and disciplining, the Militia, and for governing such Part of them as may be employed in the Service of the United States, reserving to the States respectively, the Appointment of the Officers, and the Authority of training the Militia according to the discipline prescribed by Congress;

To exercise exclusive Legislation in all Cases whatsoever, over such District (not exceeding ten Miles square) as may, by Cession of particular States, and the Acceptance of Congress, become the Seat of the Government of the United States, and to exercise like Authority over all Places purchased by the Consent of the Legislature of the State in which the Same shall be, for the Erection of Forts, Magazines, Arsenals, dock-Yards, and other needful Buildings; —And

To make all Laws which shall be necessary and proper for carrying into Execution the foregoing Powers, and all other Powers vested by this Constitution in the Government of the United States, or in any Department or Officer thereof.

What it means

Article I, Section 8 specifies the powers of Congress in great detail. These powers are limited to those listed and those that are "necessary and proper" to carry them out. All other lawmaking powers are left to the states. The First Congress, concerned that the limited nature of the federal government was not clear enough in the original Constitution, later adopted Amendment X, which reserves to the states or to the people all the powers not specifically granted to the federal government.

The most important of the specific powers that the Constitution enumerates is the power to set taxes, tariffs, and other means of raising federal revenue, and to authorize the expenditure of all federal funds. In addition to the tax powers in Article I, Amendment XVI authorized Congress to establish a national income tax. The power to appropriate federal funds is known as the "power of the purse." It gives Congress great authority over the executive branch, which must appeal to Congress for all of its funding. The federal government borrows money by issuing bonds. This creates a national debt, which the United States is obligated to repay.

Since the turn of the twentieth century, federal legislation has dealt with many matters that had previously been managed by the states. In passing these laws, Congress often relies on power granted by the commerce clause, which allows Congress to regulate business activities "among the states." The commerce clause gives Congress broad power to regulate many aspects of our economy and to pass environmental or consumer protections since so much of business today, either in manufacturing or distribution, crosses state lines. But the commerce clause powers are not unlimited. In recent years, the Supreme Court has expressed greater concern for states' rights. It has issued a series of rulings that limit the power of Congress to pass legislation under the commerce clause or other powers contained in Article I, Section 8. For example, these rulings have found unconstitutional federal laws aimed at protecting battered women or protecting schools from gun violence on the ground that these types of police matters are properly managed by the states.

In addition, Congress has the power to coin money, create the postal service, army, navy and lower federal courts and to declare war. Congress also has the responsibility of determining naturalization—how immigrants become citizens. Such laws must apply uniformly and cannot be modified by the states.

Article I, Section 9

The Migration or Importation of such Persons as any of the States now existing shall think proper to admit, shall not be prohibited by the Congress prior to the Year one thousand eight hundred and eight, but a Tax or duty may be imposed on such Importation, not exceeding ten dollars for each Person.

The Privilege of the Writ of Habeas Corpus shall not be suspended, unless when in Cases of Rebellion or Invasion the public Safety may require it.

No Bill of Attainder or ex post facto Law shall be passed.

No Capitation, or other direct, Tax shall be laid, [unless in Proportion to the Census or Enumeration herein before directed to be taken.]⁵

No Tax or Duty shall be laid on Articles exported from any State.

No Preference shall be given by any Regulation of Commerce or Revenue to the Ports of one State over those of another: nor shall Vessels bound to, or from, one State, be obliged to enter, clear, or pay Duties in another.

No Money shall be drawn from the Treasury, but in Consequence of Appropriations made by Law; and a regular Statement and Account of the Receipts and Expenditures of all public Money shall be published from time to time.

No Title of Nobility shall be granted by the United States: And no Person holding any Office of Profit or Trust under them, shall, without the Consent of the Congress, accept of any present, Emolument, Office, or Title, of any kind whatever, from any King, Prince, or foreign State.

What it means

Article I, Section 9 specifically prohibits Congress from legislating in certain areas. In the first clause, the Constitution bars Congress from banning the importation of slaves before 1808.

5. Modified by Amendment XVI.

In the second and third clauses, the Constitution specifically guarantees rights to those accused of crimes. It provides that the privilege of a writ of habeas corpus, which allows a prisoner to challenge his or her imprisonment in court, cannot be suspended except in extreme circumstances such as rebellion or invasion, where the public is in danger. Suspension of the writ of habeas corpus has occurred only a few times in history. For example, President Lincoln suspended the writ during the Civil War. In 1871, it was suspended in nine counties in South Carolina to combat the Ku Klux Klan.

Similarly, the Constitution specifically prohibits bills of attainder—laws that are directed against a specific person or group of persons, making them automatically guilty of serious crimes, such as treason, without a normal court proceeding. The ban is intended to prevent Congress from bypassing the courts and denying criminal defendants the protections guaranteed by other parts of the Constitution. In addition, the Constitution prohibits "ex post facto" laws—criminal laws that make an action illegal after someone has already taken it. This protection guarantees that individuals are warned ahead of time that their actions are illegal.

The provision in the fourth clause prohibiting states from imposing direct taxes was changed by Amendment XVI, which gives Congress the power to impose a federal income tax. In order to ensure equality among the states, the Constitution prohibits states from imposing taxes on goods coming into their state from another state and from favoring the ports of one state over the ports of others.

Article I, Section 9 also requires that Congress produce a regular accounting of the monies the federal government spends. Rejecting the monarchy of England, the Constitution also specifically prohibits Congress from granting a title of nobility to any person and prohibits public officials from accepting a title of nobility, office, or gift from any foreign country or monarch without Congressional approval.

Article I, Section 10

No State shall enter into any Treaty, Alliance, or Confederation; grant Letters of Marque and Reprisal; coin Money; emit Bills of Credit; make any Thing but gold and silver Coin a Tender in Payment of Debts; pass any Bill of Attainder, ex post facto Law, or Law impairing the Obligation of Contracts, or grant any Title of Nobility.

No State shall, without the Consent of the Congress, lay any Imposts or Duties on Imports or Exports, except what may be absolutely necessary for executing it's inspection Laws: and the net Produce of all Duties and Imposts, laid by any State on Imports or Exports, shall be for the Use of the Treasury of the United States; and all such Laws shall be subject to the Revision and Controul of the Congress.

No State shall, without the Consent of Congress, lay any Duty of Tonnage, keep Troops, or Ships of War in time of Peace, enter into any Agreement or Compact with another State, or with a foreign Power, or engage in War, unless actually invaded, or in such imminent Danger as will not admit of delay.

What it means

Article I, Section 10 limits the power of the states. States may not enter into a treaty with a foreign nation, since that power is given to the president, with the advice and consent of two thirds of the Senate present. States cannot make their own money nor can they grant any title of nobility. Like Congress, states are prohibited from passing laws that assign guilt to a specific person or group without court proceedings (bills of attainder), that make something illegal retroactively (ex post facto laws) or that interfere with legal contracts.

No state, without approval from Congress, may collect taxes on imports or exports, build an army or keep warships in times of peace, nor otherwise engage in war unless invaded or in imminent danger.

Article II, Section 1

The executive Power shall be vested in a President of the United States of America. He shall hold his Office during the Term of four Years, and, together with the Vice President, chosen for the same Term, be elected, as follows:

Each State shall appoint, in such Manner as the Legislature thereof may direct, a Number of Electors, equal to the whole Number of Senators and Representatives to which the State may be entitled in the Congress: but no Senator or Representative, or Person holding an Office of Trust or Profit under the United States, shall be appointed an Elector.

[The Electors shall meet in their respective States, and vote by Ballot for two Persons, of whom one at least shall not be an Inhabitant of the same State with themselves. And they shall make a List of all the Persons voted for, and of the Number of Votes for each; which List they shall sign and certify, and transmit sealed to the Seat of the Government of the United States, directed to the President of the Senate. The President of the Senate shall, in the Presence of the Senate and House of Representatives, open all the Certificates, and the Votes shall then be counted. The Person having the greatest Number of Votes shall be the President, if such Number be a Majority of the whole Number of Electors appointed; and if there be more than one who have such Majority, and have an equal Number of Votes, then the House of Representatives shall immediately chuse by Ballot one of them for President; and if no Person have a Majority, then from the five highest on the List the said House shall in like Manner chuse the President. But in chusing the President, the Votes shall be taken by States, the Representation from each State having one Vote; A quorum for this Purpose shall consist of a Member or Members from two thirds of the States, and a Majority of all the States shall be necessary to a Choice. In every Case, after the

Choice of the President, the Person having the greatest Number of Votes of the Electors shall be the Vice President. But if there should remain two or more who have equal Votes, the Senate shall chuse from them by Ballot the Vice President.][6]

The Congress may determine the Time of chusing the Electors, and the Day on which they shall give their Votes; which Day shall be the same throughout the United States.

No Person except a natural born Citizen, or a Citizen of the United States, at the time of the Adoption of this Constitution, shall be eligible to the Office of President; neither shall any person be eligible to that Office who shall not have attained to the Age of thirty five Years, and been fourteen Years a Resident within the United States.

[In Case of the Removal of the President from Office, or of his Death, Resignation, or Inability to discharge the Powers and Duties of the said Office, the Same shall devolve on the Vice-President, and the Congress may by Law provide for the Case of Removal, Death, Resignation or Inability, both of the President and Vice President, declaring what Officer shall then act as President, and such Officer shall act accordingly, until the Disability be removed, or a President shall be elected.][7]

The President shall, at stated Times, receive for his Services, a Compensation, which shall neither be increased nor diminished during the Period for which he shall have been elected, and he shall not receive within that Period any other Emolument from the United States, or any of them.

Before he enter on the Execution of his Office, he shall take the following Oath or Affirmation: —"I do solemnly swear (or affirm) that I will faithfully execute the Office of President of the United States, and will to the best of my Ability, preserve, protect and defend the Constitution of the United States."

6. Modified by Amendment XII.
7. Modified by Amendment XXV.

What it means

Article II, Section 1 establishes that the president has the power to run the executive branch of the government. This section, later modified by Amendments XII and XXV, outlines who is eligible to serve as president, establishes the Electoral College (the means by which the president and vice president are elected), and authorizes Congress to determine who will replace the president and vice president should they be unable to serve during their term of office.

Article II, Section 1 establishes that the president and vice president are to be elected at the same time and serve the same four-year term. Until 1951, presidents could serve for as many four-year terms as they could win. But after President Franklin D. Roosevelt was elected for four terms, Congress passed and the states ratified Amendment XXII, which limits a president to two terms (eight years) in office. In the rare case that a vice president (or other official) takes over for a president who has stepped down or died in office and serves more than two years of the remaining term, he or she is limited to one new term.

Rather than being elected directly by the people, the president is elected by members of the Electoral College, which is created by Article II, Section 1. It is not really a "college," but a group of people who are elected by the states. Each state is entitled to the number of electors equal to the combined number of their representatives and senators in Congress. Neither members of Congress nor other federal officials may serve as electors. Each state legislature decides how members of the Electoral College are to be selected and how they are to vote. For example, some states select electors at primary elections or at caucuses. In most states, electors vote for the presidential candidate that won the vote in their state. But in a few states, state law specifies that electors cast their votes according to the percentage of votes received by each candidate. If the Republican candidate receives 55% of the vote, he or she receives the votes of 55% of the electors. The creation of the Electoral College gives more power to the smaller states, rather than letting the people in the most populous states control who becomes president. Additional rules were added in 1804, when Amendment XII was adopted. For example, the amendment creates the way a president is selected when neither candidate obtains a majority of votes in the Electoral College.

There are three minimum requirements to be elected president: one must be a natural born citizen of the United States; must have lived in the United States for at least fourteen years, and must be at least thirty-five years old.

Although Article II, Section 1 originally provided who should become president if the president dies, resigns, or is removed from office, Amendment XXV, added in 1967, modified the line of succession.

The president's salary is set by Congress. To avoid allowing Congress to punish or reward the president while he or she is in office, the Constitution prohibits any change in salary during the president's term. The president also is prohibited from receiving any other type of compensation or perks while in office.

Before assuming office, the president must swear or affirm to do his or her best to serve as the nation's leader and to uphold the United States Constitution as the law of the land.

Article II, Section 2

The President shall be Commander in Chief of the Army and Navy of the United States, and of the Militia of the several States, when called into the actual Service of the United States; he may require the Opinion, in writing, of the principal Officer in each of the executive Departments, upon any Subject relating to the Duties of their respective Offices, and he shall have Power to grant Reprieves and Pardons for Offences against the United States, except in Cases of Impeachment.

He shall have Power, by and with the Advice and Consent of the Senate, to make Treaties, provided two thirds of the Senators present concur; and he shall nominate, and by and with the Advice and Consent of the Senate, shall appoint Ambassadors, other public Ministers and Consuls, Judges of the supreme Court, and all other Officers of the United States, whose Appointments are not herein otherwise provided for, and which shall be established by Law: but the Congress may by Law vest the Appointment of such inferior Officers, as they think proper, in the President alone, in the Courts of Law, or in the Heads of Departments.

The President shall have Power to fill up all Vacancies that may happen during the Recess of the Senate, by granting Commissions which shall expire at the End of their next Session.

What it means

The president serves not only as the head of the executive branch of government, but also as the commander in chief of the armed forces (including state national guards when they are called on to serve with the federal armed forces).

As chief executive, the president runs the different executive agencies, like the Department of the Treasury or the Department of Health and Human Services.

The president has the power to pardon (let free) any person who has committed a federal crime, except in cases of impeachment.

With permission from two-thirds of the Senators present, the president can make treaties (agreements) with other countries. With the approval of a majority of senators, the president makes a number of key appointments. These include U.S. ambassadors and foreign consuls, Supreme Court Justices and federal judges, U.S. Attorneys, U.S. marshals, Cabinet officers, independent agency heads and members of regulatory commissions. To ensure that the president can fill vacancies when the Senate is not in session, the president can make any of these appointments without Senate approval, but these "recess appointments" end at the end of the next Senate session.

Congress may choose to require Senate approval of other presidential appointments or let the president, courts or department heads appoint staff and agency employees without approval by the Senate.

Article II, Section 3

He shall from time to time give to the Congress Information of the State of the Union, and recommend to their Consideration such Measures as he shall judge necessary and expedient; he may, on extraordinary Occasions, convene both Houses, or either of them, and in Case of Disagreement between them, with Respect to the Time of Adjournment, he may adjourn them to such Time as he shall think proper; he shall receive Ambassadors and other public Ministers; he shall take Care that the Laws be faithfully executed, and shall Commission all the Officers of the United States.

What it means

During his or her term, the president must report to Congress about how things are going in the country. Every president from Jefferson to Taft fulfilled this duty with a written statement submitted to Congress. But in 1913, President Wilson resumed President Washington's practice of directly addressing a joint session of Congress. This "State of the Union" speech, a tradition which continues to this day, usually occurs in January or February each year.

The president also has the power, in extreme cases, to call both the House of Representatives and the Senate together for a special session. The president is given the power to meet with representatives from other nations on behalf of the United States and to otherwise run the country by enforcing the laws and directing officers and staff.

Article II, Section 4

The President, Vice President and all civil Officers of the United States, shall be removed from Office on Impeachment for, and Conviction of, Treason, Bribery, or other high Crimes and Misdemeanors.

What it means

The Constitution provides that the president, vice president, and other federal officers can be removed from office upon impeachment by the House and conviction by the Senate of treason, bribery, or other serious crimes. The process was begun only three times in U.S. history against a president—against President Andrew Johnson, President Richard Nixon (although he resigned before Congress could formally act), and President William Jefferson Clinton. The impeachment process begins in the House of Representatives with a vote to impeach. Then the president (or other accused government official) stands trial for the accusations in the Senate. The Chief Justice of the Supreme Court presides at an impeachment trial of the president. In all impeachment trials, members of the House serve as prosecutors and the full Senate sits as the jury. The accused official must be convicted by a two-thirds vote of the Senate to be removed from office.

Article III, Section 1

The judicial Power of the United States shall be vested in one supreme Court and in such inferior Courts as the Congress may from time to time ordain and establish. The Judges, both of the supreme and inferior Courts, shall hold their Offices during good Behaviour, and shall, at stated Times, receive for their Services, a Compensation, which shall not be diminished during their Continuance in Office.

What it means

Article III establishes the federal court system. The first section creates the U.S. Supreme Court as the federal system's highest court. The Supreme Court has final say on matters of federal law that come before it. Today, the U.S. Supreme Court has nine justices who are appointed by the president with the approval of the Senate.

Congress has the power to create and organize the lower federal courts. Today, there are lower federal courts in every state. A case is filed and tried in the federal district courts and in some specialty courts, like admiralty or bankruptcy courts. The trial courts look at the facts of the case and decide guilt or innocence or which side is right in an argument or dispute. The courts of appeal hear appeals of the losing parties. The appellate courts look at whether the trial was fair, whether the process followed the rules, and whether the law was correctly applied.

To assure that they are insulated from political influence, federal judges are appointed for life as long as they are on "good behavior." This generally means for as long as they want the job or until they are impeached for committing a serious crime. In addition, the Constitution specifies that Congress cannot cut a judge's pay. This prevents members of Congress from punishing a judge when they do not like one of his or her decisions.

Article III, Section 2

The judicial Power shall extend to all Cases, in Law and Equity, arising under this Constitution, the Laws of the United States, and Treaties made, or which shall be made, under their Authority;—to all Cases affecting Ambassadors, other public Ministers and Consuls;—to all Cases of admiralty and maritime Jurisdiction;—to Controversies to which the United States shall be a Party;—to Controversies between two or more States;—[between a State and

Citizens of another State;-][8] between citizens of different
States;—between Citizens of the same State claiming Lands
under Grants of different States [and between a State,
or the Citizens thereof;—and foreign States, Citizens
or Subjects.][9]

In all Cases affecting Ambassadors, other public
Ministers and Consuls, and those in which a State shall be
Party, the supreme Court shall have original Jurisdiction. In
all other Cases before mentioned, the supreme Court shall
have appellate Jurisdiction, both as to Law and Fact, with
such Exceptions, and under such Regulations as the
Congress shall make.

The Trial of all Crimes, except in Cases of Impeachment,
shall be by Jury; and such Trial shall be held in the State
where the said Crimes shall have been committed; but when
not committed within any State, the Trial shall be at such
Place or Places as the Congress may by Law have directed.

What it means

The federal courts will decide arguments over how to
interpret the Constitution, all laws passed by Congress, and
our nation's rights and responsibilities in agreements with
other nations. In addition, federal courts can hear disputes
that may arise between states, between citizens of different
states and between states and the federal government.

In 1803, in the case of *Marbury* v. *Madison*, the Supreme
Court, in an opinion written by Chief Justice John Marshall,
interpreted Article III and Article VI to give the federal
courts final say over the meaning of the federal Constitution
and federal laws and the power to order state and federal officials to comply with its rulings. The federal courts can only
make decisions on cases that are brought to them by a person
who is actually affected by the law. Federal courts are not
allowed to create cases on their own—even if they believe
a law is unconstitutional nor are they allowed to rule on
hypothetical scenarios.

8. Modified by Amendment XI.
9. Modified by Amendment XI.

Almost all federal cases start in federal district courts, where motions are decided and trials held. The cases are then heard on appeal by the federal courts of appeal and then by the Supreme Court if four justices of the nine-member Court decide to hear the case. Congress can limit the power of the appeals courts by changing the rules about which cases can be appealed. State cases that involve an issue of federal law can also be heard by the Supreme Court after the highest court in the state rules (or refuses to rule) in the case. The Supreme Court accepts only a small number of cases for review, typically around eighty cases each year. In a small number of lawsuits—those involving ambassadors, public ministers and consuls, or where a state is a party—the Supreme Court is the first court to hear the case.

The federal courts also have final say over guilt or innocence in federal criminal cases. A defendant in a criminal case, except impeachment, has a right to have his or her case heard by a jury in the state where the crime occurred.

Article III, Section 3

Treason against the United States, shall consist only in levying War against them, or in adhering to their Enemies, giving them Aid and Comfort. No person shall be convicted of Treason unless on the Testimony of two Witnesses to the same overt Act, or on Confession in open Court.

The Congress shall have Power to declare the Punishment of Treason, but no Attainder of Treason shall work Corruption of Blood, or Forfeiture except during the Life of the Person attainted.

What it means

Treason is the only crime specifically defined in the Constitution. According to Article III, Section 3, a person is guilty of treason if he or she goes to war against the United States or gives "aid or comfort" to an enemy. He or she does not have to physically pick up a weapon and fight in combat against U.S. troops. Actively helping the enemy by passing along classified information or supplying weapons, for example, can lead to charges of treason. Vocal opposition to a U.S. war effort through protest and demonstration, however, is protected by the free speech clause in Amendment I. A conviction of treason must be based either on an admission of guilt in open court or on the testimony of two witnesses. Congress may set the punishment, but it must be directed only at the guilty person and not at his or her friends or family if they were not involved in the crime.

Article IV, Section 1

Full Faith and Credit shall be given in each State to the public Acts, Records, and judicial Proceedings of every other State. And the Congress may by general Laws prescribe the Manner in which such Acts, Records and Proceedings shall be proved, and the Effect thereof.

What it means

Article IV, Section 1 ensures that states respect and honor the state laws and court orders of other states, even when their own laws are different. For example, if citizens of New Jersey marry, divorce, or adopt children in New Jersey, Florida must recognize these actions as valid even if the marriage or divorce would not have been possible under Florida law. Similarly, if a court in one state orders a person to pay money or to stop a certain behavior, the courts in other states must recognize and enforce that state's order.

Article IV, Section 1 also gives Congress the power to determine how states recognize records and laws from other states and how they enforce each others' court orders. For example, Congress may pass a federal law that specifies how states must handle child custody disputes when state laws are different or that sets out the process by which a person winning a lawsuit in one state can enforce the order in another state.

Article IV, Section 2

The Citizens of each State shall be entitled to all Privileges and Immunities of Citizens in the several States.

A Person charged in any State with Treason, Felony, or other Crime, who shall flee from Justice, and be found in another State, shall on Demand of the executive Authority of the State from which he fled, be delivered up, to be removed to the State having Jurisdiction of the Crime.

[No Person held to Service or Labour in one State, under the Laws thereof, escaping into another, shall, in Consequence of any Law or Regulation therein, be discharged from such Service or Labour, but shall be delivered up on Claim of the Party to whom such Service or Labour may be due.][10]

What it means

Article IV, Section 2 guarantees that states cannot discriminate against citizens of other states. States must give people from other states the same fundamental rights it gives its own citizens. For example, Arizona cannot prohibit New Mexico residents from traveling, owning property, or working in Arizona, nor can the state impose substantially different taxes on residents and nonresidents. But certain distinctions between residents and nonresidents—such as giving state residents a right to buy a hunting license at a lower cost—are permitted.

Article IV, Section 2 also establishes rules for when an alleged criminal flees to another state. It provides that the second state is obligated to return the fugitive to the state where the crime was committed. The process used to return fugitives (extradition) was first created by Congress and originally enforced by the governors of each state. Today courts enforce the return of accused prisoners. Fugitives do not need to have been charged with the crime in the first state in order to be captured in the second and sent back. Once returned,

10. Modified by Amendment XIII.

the state can charge the accused with any crime for which there is evidence. In contrast, when a foreign country returns a fugitive to a state for trial, the state is only allowed to try the fugitive on the charges named in the extradition papers (the formal, written request for the fugitive's return).

The fugitives from labor provision gave slave owners a nearly absolute right to recapture runaway slaves who fled to another state, even if slavery was outlawed in that state. This also meant that state laws in free states intended to protect runaway slaves were unconstitutional because they interfered with the slave owner's right to the slave's return. The adoption of Amendment XIII, which abolishes slavery and prohibits involuntary servitude, nullified this provision.

Article IV, Section 3

New States may be admitted by the Congress into this Union; but no new State shall be formed or erected within the Jurisdiction of any other State; nor any State be formed by the Junction of two or more States, or Parts of States, without the Consent of the Legislatures of the States concerned as well as of the Congress.

The Congress shall have Power to dispose of and make all needful Rules and Regulations respecting the Territory or other Property belonging to the United States; and nothing in this Constitution shall be so construed as to Prejudice any Claims of the United States, or of any particular State.

What it means

Congress can admit new states into the Union, but a single state cannot create a new state within its boundaries. For example, the state of New York cannot make New York City a separate state. In addition, two states, or parts of states (i.e. Oregon and Idaho or Wilmington, Delaware, and Philadelphia, Pennsylvania) cannot become states without the consent of the various state legislatures and Congress. Although an original version of the Constitution included a requirement that each new state join the Union on equal footing with the other states, the language was removed before the document was approved. Nevertheless, Congress has always granted new states rights equal to those of existing states.

Not all of the lands that are owned or controlled by the United States are states. Some lands are territories, and Congress has the power to sell off or regulate the territories. This includes allowing U.S. territories to become independent nations, as was done with the Philippines, or regulating the affairs of current U.S. territories like the District of Columbia, Guam, or Puerto Rico. In addition, this provision gives Congress the power to set rules for lands owned by the United States, such as the national parks and national forests. The last sentence of this clause makes sure that nothing in the Constitution would harm the rights of either the federal government or the states in disputes over property.

Article IV, Section 4

The United States shall guarantee to every State in this Union a Republican Form of Government, and shall protect each of them against Invasion; and on Application of the Legislature, or of the Executive (when the Legislature cannot be convened) against domestic Violence.

What it means

This provision, known as the guarantee clause, is attributed to James Madison. It has not been widely interpreted, but scholars think it ensures that each state be run as a representative democracy, as opposed to a monarchy (run by a king or queen) or a dictatorship (where one individual or group of individuals controls the government). Courts however have been reluctant to specify what exactly a republican form of government means, leaving that decision exclusively to Congress.

The section also gives Congress the power (and obligation) to protect the states from an invasion by a foreign country, or from significant violent uprisings within each state. It authorizes the legislature of each state (or the executive, if the legislature cannot be assembled in time) to request federal help with riots or other violence.

Article V

The Congress, whenever two thirds of both Houses shall deem it necessary, shall propose Amendments to this Constitution, or, on the Application of the Legislatures of two thirds of the several States, shall call a Convention for proposing Amendments, which, in either Case, shall be valid to all Intents and Purposes, as Part of this Constitution, when ratified by the Legislatures of three fourths of the several States, or by Conventions in three fourths thereof, as the one or the other Mode of Ratification may be proposed by the Congress; Provided that no Amendment which may be made prior to the Year One thousand eight hundred and eight shall in any Manner affect the first and fourth Clauses in the Ninth Section of the first Article; and that no State, without its Consent, shall be deprived of its equal Suffrage in the Senate.

What it means

Realizing that over time the nation may want to make changes to the Constitution, Article V establishes the amendment process. But unlike laws and regulations, which can be passed or amended by a simple majority of those voting in Congress, the Constitution is difficult to change. An amendment can be offered in one of two ways: when two-thirds of the Senate (67 of 100 senators) and two-thirds of the House of Representatives (290 of 435 representatives) call for a change to be made; or when two-thirds of the states (34 of 50 states) call for a national constitutional convention (a gathering of representatives of each state) to make a change.

Once the amendment is proposed, three-fourths of the state legislatures or state conventions (38 of 50 states) must vote to approve (ratify) the change. An amendment becomes effective when the necessary states have ratified it.

The article also forbids three specific amendments: that would deny a state its votes in the Senate, that before 1808 would enable Congress to prohibit the importation of slaves and that before 1808 would allow direct taxation except as based on the system of enumeration set out in Article I, Section 2. As a result, the three-fifths compromise contained in Article I, Section 9 remained in place until 1808 when Congress banned the international slave trade.

Article VI

All Debts contracted and Engagements entered into, before the Adoption of this Constitution, shall be as valid against the United States under this Constitution, as under the Confederation.

This Constitution, and the Laws of the United States which shall be made in Pursuance thereof; and all Treaties made, or which shall be made, under the Authority of the United States, shall be the supreme Law of the Land; and the Judges in every State shall be bound thereby, any Thing in the Constitution or Laws of any State to the Contrary notwithstanding.

The Senators and Representatives before mentioned, and the Members of the several State Legislatures, and all executive and judicial Officers, both of the United States and of the several States, shall be bound by Oath or Affirmation, to support this Constitution; but no religious Test shall ever be required as a Qualification to any Office or public Trust under the United States.

What it means

Often referred to as the supremacy clause, this article says that when state law is in conflict with federal law, federal law must prevail. Because of the great number of federal and state laws, many of which deal with the same or similar topics, there have been many lawsuits claiming that state laws conflict with federal laws and are therefore invalid. In these lawsuits, the Supreme Court generally looks at whether Congress has established a national regulatory scheme and if so, states cannot regulate in that area. The Court also looks at whether the state law directly interferes or is in conflict with federal law. In all of these cases, the supremacy clause ensures that federal law takes priority over, or preempts, state law. The prioritizing of federal over state powers is known as the "doctrine of preemption."

Article VI also provides that both federal and state officials—including legislators and judges—must obey the U.S. Constitution (state officials have a duty to obey their own state constitutions and laws as well). To ensure freedom of religion, this article ensures that no public official be required to practice or pledge allegiance to any particular religion.

Article VII

The Ratification of the Conventions of nine States, shall be sufficient for the Establishment of this Constitution between the States so ratifying the Same.

What it means

All of the states, except Rhode Island held conventions to ratify the Constitution, although North Carolina's convention adjourned without voting on the document. Delaware was the first state to ratify the Constitution in 1787 and New Hampshire became the ninth state to ratify on June 21, 1788. The new government began with the convening of the first federal Congress on March 4, 1789. Both North Carolina (in

1789) and Rhode Island (in 1790) ratified the Constitution after Congress passed the Bill of Rights and sent it to the states for ratification.

Done in Convention by the Unanimous Consent of the States present the Seventeenth Day of September in the Year of our Lord one thousand seven hundred and Eighty seven and of the Independence of the United States of America the Twelfth In witness whereof We have hereunto subscribed our Names,

Gº WASHINGTON—
Presidt. and deputy from Virginia

[Signed also by the deputies of twelve States.]

New Hampshire	John Langdon
	Nicholas Gilman
Massachusetts	Nathaniel Gorham
	Rufus King
Connecticut	Wm. Saml. Johnson
	Roger Sherman
New York	Alexander Hamilton
New Jersey	Wil: Livingston
	David Brearley
	Wm. Paterson
	Jona: Dayton
Pennsylvania	B Franklin
	Thomas Mifflin
	Robt Morris
	Geo. Clymer
	Thos. FitzSimons
	Jared Ingersoll
	James Wilson
	Gouv Morris

Delaware	Geo: Read
	Gunning Bedford jun
	John Dickinson
	Richard Bassett
	Jaco: Broom
Maryland	James McHenry
	Dan of St. Thos. Jenifer
	Danl Carroll
Virginia	John Blair—
	James Madison Jr.
North Carolina	Wm. Blount
	Richd. Dobbs Spaight
	Hu Williamson
South Carolina	J. Rutledge
	Charles Cotesworth Pinckney
	Charles Pinckney
	Pierce Butler
Georgia	William Few
	Abr Baldwin

Attest William Jackson Secretary

AMENDMENTS TO THE CONSTITUTION OF THE UNITED STATES OF AMERICA

Amendment I[11]

Congress shall make no law respecting an establishment of religion, or prohibiting the free exercise thereof; or abridging the freedom of speech, or of the press; or the right of the people peaceably to assemble, and to petition the Government for a redress of grievances.

What it means

Freedom of Speech and of the Press: The First Amendment allows citizens to express and to be exposed to a wide range of opinions and views. It was intended to ensure a free exchange of ideas even if the ideas are unpopular. Freedom of speech encompasses not only the spoken and written word, but also all kinds of expression (including non-verbal communications, like sit-ins, art, photographs, films and advertisements). Under its provisions the media—including television, radio, and the Internet—is free to distribute a wide range of news, facts, opinions, and pictures. The amendment protects not only the speaker, but also the person who receives the information. The right to read, hear, see and obtain different points of view is a First Amendment right as well.

But the right to free speech is not absolute. The Supreme Court has ruled that the government sometimes may be allowed to limit speech. For example, the government may limit or ban libel (the communication of false statements about a person that may injure his or her reputation),

11. On September 25, 1789, Congress transmitted to the states twelve proposed amendments. Two of these, which involved congressional representation and pay, were not adopted. The remaining ten amendments, known as the Bill of Rights, were ratified on December 15, 1791.

obscenity, fighting words, and words that present a clear and present danger of causing violence. The government also may regulate speech by limiting the time, place or manner in which it is made. For example the government may require activists to obtain a permit before holding a large protest rally on a public street.

Freedom of Assembly and Right to Petition the Government: The First Amendment also protects the freedom of assembly, which can mean physically gathering with a group of people to picket or protest; or associating with one another in groups for economic, political, or religious purposes. The First Amendment also protects the right not to associate, which means that the government cannot force people to join a group they do not wish to join. A related right is the right to petition the government, including everything from signing a petition to filing a lawsuit.

Freedom of Religion: The First Amendment's free exercise clause allows a person to hold whatever religious beliefs he or she wants, and to exercise that belief by attending religious services, praying in public or in private, proselytizing or wearing religious clothing such as yarmulkes or headscarves. Also included in the free exercise clause is the right not to believe in any religion, and the right not to participate in religious activities.

Second, the establishment clause prevents the government from creating a church, endorsing religion in general, or favoring one set of religious beliefs over another. As the Supreme Court decided in 1947 in *Everson v. Board of Education of Ewing Township*, the establishment clause was intended to erect "a wall of separation between church and state," although the degree to which government should accomodate religion in public life has been debated in numerous Supreme Court decisions since then.

Amendment II

A well regulated Militia, being necessary to the security of a free State, the right of the people to keep and bear Arms, shall not be infringed.

What it means

Right to Bear Arms: The principal debate surrounding the Second Amendment concerns whether the right to use and buy guns belongs to individuals or only to a militia. Although the courts generally have held that the right applies to individuals, they have permitted the government to limit some rights of gun manufacturers, owners and sellers. Today, questions about the Second Amendment center around bans on assault weapons, mandatory background checks, waiting periods, and other restrictions on gun sales or use.

With the passage of the Fourteenth Amendment and subsequent Supreme Court rulings, states were prohibited from making or enforcing laws that infringe on most of the rights set out in the Bill of Rights. However, this prohibition does not extend to the Second Amendment. This means that the Second Amendment applies only to actions by the federal government. It does not protect people from state actions that interfere with their right to bear arms. As a result, gun control legislation varies widely among the fifty states.

Amendment III

No Soldier shall, in time of peace be quartered in any house, without the consent of the Owner, nor in time of war, but in a manner to be prescribed by law.

What it means

The Third Amendment is intended to protect citizens' rights to the ownership and use of their property without intrusion by the government. The drafters of the Constitution, like many other colonists, were resentful of laws, in place before the Revolutionary War, that allowed British soldiers to take over private homes for their own use. Thus, the amendment bars the government from forcing individuals to provide lodging to soldiers in their homes, except during war when the interest of national security may override an individual's right of private property.

Rarely discussed in detail in Supreme Court decisions, the Third Amendment has more commonly been held up as evidence that the framers meant the Constitution to protect individuals from government intrusion into their homes, family lives and personal affairs.

Amendment IV

The right of the people to be secure in their persons, houses, papers, and effects, against unreasonable searches and seizures, shall not be violated, and no Warrants shall issue, but upon probable cause, supported by Oath or affirmation, and particularly describing the place to be searched, and the persons or things to be seized.

What it means

Protection against Unreasonable Search and Seizure: The Fourth Amendment protects people against unreasonable searches and seizures by government officials. A search can mean everything from a frisking by a police officer to a blood test to a search of an individual's home or car. A seizure occurs when the government takes control of an individual or something in his or her possession. Items that are seized often are used as evidence when the individual is charged with a crime.

The Fourth Amendment imposes certain limitations on police investigating a crime and prevents the use of illegally obtained evidence at trial. But it does not restrict all searches. For example, courts have ruled that school officials may search school lockers and require that students who participate in extracurricular activities undergo random drug testing.

Amendment V

No person shall be held to answer for a capital, or otherwise infamous crime, unless on a presentment or indictment of a Grand Jury, except in cases arising in the land or naval forces, or in the Militia, when in actual service in time of War or public danger; nor shall any person be subject for the same offence to be twice put in jeopardy of life or limb; nor shall be compelled in any criminal case to be a witness against himself, nor be deprived of life, liberty, or property, without due process of law; nor shall private property be taken for public use, without just compensation.

What it means

Grand Jury Protection: The Fifth Amendment requirement that serious federal criminal charges be started by a grand jury (a group of citizens who hear evidence from a prosecutor about potential crimes) is rooted in English common law. Its basic purpose is to provide a fair method for beginning criminal proceedings against those accused of committing crimes. Grand jury charges can be issued against anyone except members of the military, who are instead subject to courts - martial in the military justice system.

To avoid giving government unchecked powers, grand jurors are selected from the general population and their work, conducted in secret, is not hampered by rigid rules about the type of evidence that can be heard. In fact, grand jurors can act on their own knowledge and are free to start criminal proceedings on any information that they think relevant. It is these broad powers that have led some critics to charge that grand juries are little more than puppets of prosecutors. Grand juries also serve an investigative role because grand juries can compel witnesses to testify in the absence of their lawyers.

A significant number of states do not use grand juries, instead they begin criminal proceedings using informations or indictments. The right to a grand jury is one of only a few protections in the Bill of Rights that has not been applied to the states by the Fourteenth Amendment.

Protection against Double Jeopardy: This portion of the Fifth Amendment protects individuals from being "twice put in jeopardy of life or limb"—that is, in danger of being punished more than once for the same criminal act. The U.S. Supreme Court has interpreted the double jeopardy clause to protect against a second prosecution for the same offense after acquittal or conviction and against multiple punishments for the same crime. Like other provisions in the Bill of Rights that affect criminal prosecutions, the double jeopardy clause is rooted in the idea that the government should not have unlimited power to prosecute and punish criminal suspects. Rather, government gets only one chance to make its case.

Right against Self-Incrimination: This provision of the Fifth Amendment is probably the best-known of all constitutional rights, as it appears frequently on television and in movies—whether in dramatic courtroom scenes ("I take the Fifth!") or before the police question someone in their custody ("You have the right to remain silent. Anything you do say can be used against you in a court of law."). The right protects a person from being forced to reveal to the police, prosecutor, judge, or jury any information that might subject him or her to criminal prosecution. Even if a person is guilty of a crime, the Fifth Amendment demands that the prosecutors come up with other evidence to prove their case. If police violate the Fifth Amendment by forcing a suspect to confess, a court may suppress the confession, that is, prohibit it from being used as evidence at trial. The right to remain silent also means that a defendant has the right not to take the witness stand at all during his or her trial, and that the prosecutor cannot point to the defendant's silence as evidence of guilt.

There are, however, limitations on the right against self-incrimination. For example, it applies only to testimonial acts, such as speaking, nodding, or writing. Other personal information that might be incriminating, like blood or hair samples, DNA or fingerprints, may be used as evidence. Similarly, incriminating statements that an individual makes voluntarily—

such as when a suspect confesses to a friend or writes in a personal diary—are not protected.

Right to Due Process: The right to due process of law has been recognized since 1215, when the Magna Carta (the British charter) was adopted. Historically, the right protected people accused of crimes from being imprisoned without fair procedures (like indictments and trials, where they would have an opportunity to confront their accusers). The right of due process has grown in two directions: It affords individuals a right to a fair process (known as procedural due process) and a right to enjoy certain fundamental liberties without governmental interference (known as substantive due process). The Fifth Amendment's due process clause applies to the federal government's conduct. In 1868 the adoption of the Fourteenth Amendment expanded the right of due process to include limits on the actions of state governments. Today, court decisions interpreting the Fourteenth Amendment's due process right generally apply to the Fifth Amendment and vice versa.

Takings Clause: The takings clause of the Fifth Amendment strikes a balance between the rights of private property owners and the right of the government to take that property for a purpose that benefits the public at large. When the government takes private property, it is required to pay just compensation to the property owner for his or her loss. The takings power of the government, sometimes referred to as the power of eminent domain, may be used for a wide range of valid public uses (for a highway or a park, for example). For the most part, when defining just compensation, courts try to reach some approximation of market value.

Amendment VI

In all criminal prosecutions, the accused shall enjoy the right to a speedy and public trial, by an impartial jury of the State and district wherein the crime shall have been committed; which district shall have been previously ascertained by law, and to be informed of the nature and

cause of the accusation; to be confronted with the witnesses against him; to have compulsory process for obtaining witnesses in his favor, and to have the assistance of counsel for his defence.

What it means

Right to a Jury Trial: In a criminal case, the government prosecutes or charges a defendant with a violation of the criminal law and begins proceedings (bail hearings, arraignments and trials) to prove that charge beyond a reasonable doubt. The Sixth Amendment provides many protections and rights to a person accused of a crime. One right is to have his or her case heard by an impartial jury—independent people from the surrounding community who are willing to decide the case based only on the evidence. In some cases where there has been a significant amount of news coverage, the Supreme Court has ruled that jury members may be picked from another location in order to ensure that the jurors are impartial. When choosing a jury, both prosecutors and defense attorneys may object to certain people being included. Some of these objections, called challenges, are for cause (the potential juror has said or done something that shows he or she may not act fairly). Others are peremptory (no real reason need be given, but one side does not want to have that person serve). Lawyers cannot use peremptory challenges to keep people off a jury because of race or gender.

Right to a Speedy Trial: This right is considered one of the most important in the Constitution. Without it, criminal defendants could be held indefinitely under a cloud of unproven criminal accusations. The right to a speedy trial also is crucial to assuring that a criminal defendant receives a fair trial. If too much time elapses between the alleged crime and the trial, witnesses may die or leave the area, their memories may fade, and physical evidence may be lost.

The Public Trial Guarantee: Like the right to a speedy trial, the right to a public trial serves the interests of both criminal defendants and the public. Defendants are protected from secret proceedings that might encourage abuse of the justice system, and the public is kept informed about how the criminal justice system works. Like most constitutional protections, however, the right to a public trial is not absolute. A criminal defendant may voluntarily give up (waive) his or her right to a public proceeding or the judge may limit public access in certain circumstances. For example, a judge might order a closed hearing to prevent intimidation of a witness or to keep order in the courtroom.

Right to Be Informed of Criminal Charges: The Sixth Amendment right to "be informed of the nature and cause of the accusation" is another protection meant to ensure that the accused receives a fair trail. A speedy, public trial that is heard by an impartial jury is meaningless if a defendant is left in the dark about exactly the crime with which he or she is charged.

Right to Be Confronted by Adverse Witnesses: The so-called confrontation clause prevents prosecutors from relying on witnesses' out-of-court statements to make their case. Rather, it requires that prosecutors put their witnesses on the stand, under oath. As the U.S. Supreme Court explained in its 1970 opinion, *California v. Green*, the defendant's ability to confront a hostile witness in person puts pressure on the witness to tell the truth, allows the defendant's counsel to cross-examine the witness (which may reveal him or her to be unreliable), and gives the jury an up-close view of the witness, so that they can decide for themselves if the witness is believable.

There are exceptions to the confrontation clause, of course. If a knowledgeable witness is unavailable at the time of trial, for example, a previous statement will be allowed into evidence, so long as the witness made it under conditions that were similar to those at trial (for example, if the statement was made under oath). Defendants also may be prevented from confronting witnesses against them when the well-being of the witness is at issue. For example, child witnesses may be allowed to testify in the judge's chambers rather than in open court.

Right to Assistance of Counsel: The Sixth Amendment guarantees a criminal defendant the right to have an attorney defend him or her at trial. That right is not dependent on the defendant's ability to pay an attorney; if a defendant cannot afford a lawyer, the government is required to provide one. The right to counsel is more than just the right to have an attorney physically present at criminal proceedings. The assistance provided by the attorney must be effective. This does not mean that the defendant has a right to an attorney who will win his or her case. A defendant can receive effective assistance of counsel and still be convicted and sent to jail. However, if an attorney's performance is not up to reasonable standards for the profession or if the attorney's ability to put on a full defense is hindered by the prosecutor's misconduct, then the defendant may be able to challenge his or her conviction. This provision does not guarantee the right to an attorney in most civil cases.

Amendment VII

In Suits at common law, where the value in controversy shall exceed twenty dollars, the right of trial by jury shall be preserved, and no fact tried by a jury, shall be otherwise re-examined in any Court of the United States, than according to the rules of the common law.

What it means

The Seventh Amendment extends the right to a jury trial to federal civil cases such as car accidents, disputes between corporations for breach of contract, or most discrimination or employment disputes. In civil cases, the person bringing the lawsuit (the plaintiff) seeks money damages or a court order preventing the person being sued (the defendant) from engaging in certain conduct. To win, the plaintiff must prove his or her case by "a preponderance of the evidence," that is by over fifty percent of the proof.

Although the Seventh Amendment itself says that it is limited to "suits at common law," meaning cases that triggered the right to a jury under English law, the amendment has been found to apply in lawsuits that are similar to the old common law cases. For example, the right to a jury trial applies to cases brought under federal statutes that prohibit race or gender discrimination in housing or employment. But importantly, the Seventh Amendment guarantees the right to a jury trial only in federal court, not in state court.

Amendment VIII

Excessive bail shall not be required, nor excessive fines imposed, nor cruel and unusual punishments inflicted.

What it means

No Excessive Bail: The first portion of the Eighth Amendment concerns bail—the money paid by a defendant in a criminal case in exchange for his or her release from jail before trial. Bail is returned to the defendant when he or she appears at trial but is forfeited to the government if he or she does not appear. In this way, bail provides an incentive for a defendant to remain in the area and participate in the trial. Bail also promotes the ideal of being innocent until proven guilty, in that a defendant is not punished with jail time before he or she actually has been convicted. Bail also assists a defendant in preparing his or her case for trial, for it is far more difficult to consult with counsel when one is in police custody.

The Eighth Amendment ensures that bail cannot be "excessive," at an amount so high that it would be impossible for all but the richest defendants to pay it. The Eighth Amendment however, does not guarantee an absolute right to be released on bail before trial. The U.S. Supreme Court has identified circumstances when a court may refuse bail entirely, such as when a defendant shows a significant risk of running away or poses a considerable danger to the community.

Prohibition against Cruel and Unusual Punishment: The better-known component of the Eighth Amendment is the prohibition against cruel and unusual punishment. Although this phrase originally was intended to outlaw certain gruesome methods of punishment—such as torture, burning at the stake, or crucifixion—it has been broadened over the years to protect against punishments that are grossly disproportionate to (meaning much too harsh for) the particular crime. Except for a brief period in the 1970s, the death penalty has not been considered by the U.S. Supreme Court to be cruel and unusual punishment. As a result, Eighth Amendment challenges to the death penalty have focused on the methods used to carry out executions, whether certain offenders (for example, juveniles or the mentally retarded) should be subject to the sentence and whether death sentences are decided in a fair manner and by an impartial jury.

It is not just criminal sentences themselves that are subject to the cruel and unusual test; the Eighth Amendment's cruel and unusual provision has been used to challenge prison conditions such as extremely unsanitary cells, overcrowding, insufficient medical care and deliberate failure by officials to protect inmates from one another.

Amendment IX

The enumeration in the Constitution, of certain rights, shall not be construed to deny or disparage others retained by the people.

What it means

The Ninth Amendment is a constitutional safety net intended to make clear that individuals have other fundamental rights, in addition to those listed in the First through Eighth Amendments. Some of the framers had raised concerns that because it was impossible to list every fundamental right, it would be dangerous to list just some of them (for example, the right to free speech, the right to bear arms, and so forth), for fear of suggesting that the list was complete. This group of framers opposed a bill of rights entirely and favored a more general declaration of fundamental rights. But others, including many state representatives, had refused to ratify the Constitution without a more specific list of protections, so the First Congress added the Ninth Amendment as a compromise. Because the rights protected by the Ninth Amendment are not specified, they are referred to as "unenumerated." The Supreme Court has found that unenumerated rights include such important rights as the right to travel, the right to vote, the right to keep personal matters private and to make important decisions about one's health care or body.

Amendment X

The powers not delegated to the United States by the Constitution, nor prohibited by it to the States, are reserved to the States respectively, or to the people.

What it means

The Tenth Amendment was included in the Bill of Rights to further define the balance of power between the federal government and the states. The amendment says that the federal government has only those powers specifically granted by the Constitution. These powers include the power to declare war, to collect taxes, to regulate interstate business activities and others that are listed in the articles. Any power not listed, says the Tenth Amendment, is left to the states or the people. Although the Tenth Amendment does not specify what these "powers" may be, the U.S. Supreme Court has ruled that laws affecting family relations (such as marriage, divorce, and adoption), commerce that occurs within a state's own borders, and local law enforcement activities, are among those specifically reserved to the states or the people.

Amendment XI

The Judicial power of the United States shall not be construed to extend to any suit in law or equity, commenced or prosecuted against one of the United States by Citizens of another State, or by Citizens or Subjects of any Foreign State.

What it means

After the U.S. Supreme Court ruled in 1793 that two South Carolina men could sue and collect debts from the State of Georgia, states-rights advocates in Congress and the states pushed for what became the Eleventh Amendment in 1795. The amendment specifically prohibits federal courts from hearing cases in which a state is sued by an individual from another state or another country. Protecting states from certain types of legal liability is a concept known as "sovereign immunity."

The amendment did not bar all lawsuits against states in federal courts. For example, as initially interpreted, the Eleventh Amendment did not bar suits against states when a matter of federal law was at issue nor did it prevent suits brought against a state by its own citizens. But more recently, a divided Supreme Court has held that states are immune from all lawsuits in federal courts unless they specifically agree to be sued.

Amendment XII

The Electors shall meet in their respective states, and vote by ballot for President and Vice-President, one of whom, at least, shall not be an inhabitant of the same state with themselves; they shall name in their ballots the person voted for as President, and in distinct ballots the person voted for as Vice-President, and they shall make distinct lists of all persons voted for as President, and of all persons voted for as Vice-President, and of the number of votes for each, which lists they shall sign and certify, and transmit sealed to the seat of the government of the United States, directed to the President of the Senate;—The President of the Senate shall, in the presence of the Senate and House of Representatives, open all the certificates and the votes shall then be counted;—The person having the greatest number of votes for President, shall be the President, if such number be a majority of the whole number of Electors appointed; and if no person have such majority, then from the persons having the highest numbers not exceeding three on the list of those voted for as President, the House of Representatives shall choose immediately, by ballot, the President. But in choosing the President, the votes shall be taken by states, the representation from each state having one vote; a quorum for this purpose shall consist of a member or members from two-thirds of the states, and a majority of all the states shall be necessary to a choice. [And if the House of Representatives shall not choose a President whenever the right of choice shall devolve upon them, before the fourth day of March next following, then the Vice-President shall act as President, as in the case of the death or other constitutional disability of the President.—][12] The person having the greatest number of votes as Vice-President, shall be the Vice-President, if such number be a majority of the whole number of Electors appointed, and if no person have a majority, then from the two highest numbers on the list, the Senate shall choose the Vice-President; a quorum for the purpose shall consist of two-thirds of the whole number of Senators, and a majority of the whole number shall be necessary to a choice. But no person constitutionally ineligible to the office of President shall be eligible to that of Vice-President of the United States.

What it means

Approved by Congress on December 9, 1803, and ratified by the states on June 15, 1804, the Twelfth Amendment modifies the way the Electoral College chooses the president

12. Modified by Amendment XX, Section 3.

and vice president. Article II, Section 1 of the Constitution, which established the Electoral College, provided that each state appoint electors equal to the total number of House and Senate members in their state and that the electors shall vote for two persons. The presidential candidate who received the most electoral votes won the presidency; the runner-up became the vice president. In 1796, this meant that the president and the vice president were from different parties and had different political views, making governance more difficult. The adoption of Amendment XII solved this problem by allowing each party to nominate their team for president and vice president.

The inhabitant clause of the Twelfth Amendment also suggests strongly that the president and vice president should not be from the same state. Although the provision does not directly disqualify a vice president who is from the same state as the president, the provision disqualifies the electors from that state from voting for both offices. Prior to the 2000 election, both presidential candidate George W. Bush and vice presidential candidate Dick Cheney lived in and voted in Texas. To avoid problems with the inhabitant clause, Cheney registered to vote in Wyoming, where he previously lived.

The Twelfth Amendment also specifies how the president and vice president are to be selected should neither candidate obtain the votes of a majority of the electors: the House of Representatives selects the new president from the top three candidates. This is a slight variation from the original provision, which allowed the choice from among the top five candidates. However, the vote within the House is by state, not by representative. This gives equal weight to all states— the smaller, less populated states as well as the larger, more populated ones—and makes it more likely that the ultimate winner may not be the candidate who obtains the majority of the popular vote. Lastly, this amendment extends the eligibility requirements to become president (the candidate must be a natural born citizen, must be at least thirty-five years old, and must have been a resident of the United States for fourteen years) to the vice president since no person who is constitutionally ineligible to be president can be vice president.

Amendment XIII

Section 1. Neither slavery nor involuntary servitude, except as a punishment for crime whereof the party shall have been duly convicted, shall exist within the United States, or any place subject to their jurisdiction.

Section 2. Congress shall have power to enforce this article by appropriate legislation.

What it means

In 1863, based on his war powers (see Article II, Section 2), President Lincoln issued the Emancipation Proclamation, which freed the slaves held within any designated state and part of a state in rebellion against the United States. The Proclamation provided "all persons held as slaves . . . are, and henceforward shall be free . . . ." Because the Proclamation did not address slaves held in the Northern states, there were questions about its validity. Following the end of the fighting, on February 1, 1865, Congress passed the Thirteenth Amendment and forwarded it to the states. It was ratified on December 18, 1865. The Thirteenth Amendment was the first of three Reconstruction Era amendments (the Thirteenth, Fourteenth, and Fifteenth) that eliminated slavery, guaranteed due process, equal protection and voting rights to all Americans.

By its adoption, Congress intended the Thirteenth Amendment to take the question of emancipation away from politics. The Supreme Court found in *In Re Slaughter-House Cases*, that the "word servitude is of larger meaning than slavery . . . and the obvious purpose was to forbid all shades and conditions of African slavery." Although some may have questioned whether persons other than African Americans could share in the amendment's protection, the Court held that the amendment "forbids any other kind of slavery, now or hereafter. If Mexican peonage [the practice of forcing someone to work against one's will to pay off a debt] or the Chinese coolie labor system shall develop slavery of the Mexican or Chinese race within our territory, this amendment may safely be trusted to make it void."

In more recent cases, the Supreme Court has defined involuntary servitude broadly to forbid work forced by the use or threat of physical restraint or injury or through law. But the Supreme Court has rejected claims that define mandatory community service, taxation, and the draft as involuntary servitude.

Amendment XIV

Section 1. All persons born or naturalized in the United States and subject to the jurisdiction thereof, are citizens of the United States and of the State wherein they reside. No State shall make or enforce any law which shall abridge the privileges or immunities of citizens of the United States; nor shall any State deprive any person of life, liberty, or property, without due process of law; nor deny to any person within its jurisdiction the equal protection of the laws.

Section 2. Representatives shall be apportioned among the several States according to their respective numbers, counting the whole number of persons in each State, excluding Indians not taxed. But when the right to vote at any election for the choice of electors for President and Vice President of the United States, Representatives in Congress, the Executive and Judicial officers of a State, or the members of the Legislature thereof, is denied to any of the male inhabitants of such State, being twenty-one years of age, and citizens of the United States, or in any way abridged, except for participation in rebellion, or other crime, the basis of representation therein shall be reduced in the proportion which the number of such male citizens shall bear to the whole number of male citizens twenty-one years of age in such State.

Section 3. No person shall be a Senator or Representative in Congress, or elector of President and

Vice President, or hold any office, civil or military, under the United States, or under any State, who, having previously taken an oath, as a member of Congress, or as an officer of the United States, or as a member of any State legislature, or as an executive or judicial officer of any State, to support the Constitution of the United States, shall have engaged in insurrection or rebellion against the same, or given aid or comfort to the enemies thereof. But Congress may by a vote of two-thirds of each House, remove such disability.

Section 4. The validity of the public debt of the United States, authorized by law, including debts incurred for payment of pensions and bounties for services in suppressing insurrection or rebellion, shall not be questioned. But neither the United States nor any State shall assume or pay any debt or obligation incurred in aid of insurrection or rebellion against the United States, or any claim for the loss or emancipation of any slave; but all such debts, obligations and claims shall be held illegal and void.

Section 5. The Congress shall have power to enforce, by appropriate legislation, the provisions of this article.

What it means

Because many states continued to pass laws that restricted the rights of former slaves, on June 13, 1866, Congress passed and sent to the states for ratification, Amendment XIV. Ratified on July 9, 1868, the amendment granted U.S. citizenship to former slaves and specifically changed the rule in Article 1, Section 2 that slaves be counted only as three-fifths of a person for purposes of representation in Congress. It also contained three new limits on state power: a state shall not violate a citizen's privileges or immunities; shall not deprive any person of life, liberty, or property without due process of law; and must guarantee all persons equal protection of the laws. These limitations on state power dramatically expanded the protections of the Constitution. Prior to the adoption of the Fourteenth Amendment, the protections in the Bill of Rights limited only the actions of the federal government, unless the provision specifically stated otherwise. The Supreme Court, in what is called "the doctrine of incorporation" has since interpreted the Fourteenth Amendment to apply most provisions in the Bill of Rights against state and local governments as well. This has meant that the Fourteenth Amendment has been used more frequently in modern court cases than any other constitutional provision.

Guaranteed Rights of Citizenship to all Persons Born or Naturalized: The right of citizenship in the Fourteenth Amendment was intended to overturn the case of *Dred Scott v. Sanford*, a decision that had long been considered as one of the Supreme Court's worst mistakes. Dred Scott, born into slavery, argued that he should be granted freedom from the family that claimed ownership over him because he had lived in free states and thus had become a citizen of the United States before returning to Missouri, a state where slavery was sanctioned. Chief Justice Taney, denying Scott's appeal, held that African Americans were not citizens, and therefore were "not included, and were not intended to be included, under the word citizens." By specifically granting citizenship to all persons born or naturalized, the Fourteenth Amendment has not only guaranteed citizenship to former slaves but to most children born within the United States, even if the child's parents are not and cannot become citizens.

Amendment XIV, however, limited the broad grant of citizenship to those "subject to U.S. jurisdiction." As a result, Native Americans, who were governed by tribal law, were not guaranteed citizenship by this amendment. Many Native Americans became citizens by a variety of means such as marriage, treaties, or military service. But with the passage of the Indian Citizenship Act of 1924, Congress granted the rights of citizenship to all Native Americans.

Privileges and Immunities: Within five years of its adoption, the privileges and immunities clause of the Fourteenth Amendment was interpreted very narrowly by the U.S. Supreme Court. In *In Re Slaughter-House Cases*, the

Court rejected the argument that the provision gave the federal government broad power to enforce civil rights, finding that to do so would infringe on a power that had and should belong to the states. The Court found that the only privileges protected by the clause are those "which owe their existence to the Federal Government, its National character, its Constitution, or its laws," all of which are already protected from state interference by the supremacy clause in Article VI. Subsequent cases have recognized several federal privileges such as the right to travel from state to state, the right to petition Congress for a redress of grievances, the right to vote for national officers, and so forth, but other efforts to broaden the meaning of this clause have been rejected.

Procedural Due Process: The Fourteenth Amendment's due process clause has been interpreted by the courts to provide the same "protection against arbitrary state legislation, affecting life, liberty and property, as is offered by the Fifth Amendment." This has meant that state laws that take away a person's property or otherwise jeopardize their life or liberty must afford persons a fair and impartial way to challenge that action. For example, the due process clause has ensured that people on welfare are able to challenge the loss of their benefits at an administrative hearing, and has meant that parents who are accused of child abuse, or the mentally ill who are being committed will have the opportunity to contest the state's allegations in a court hearing. Often thought of as a provision that guarantees fairness, the due process clause requires government to use even-handed procedures, so that it is less likely to act in an arbitrary way.

Substantive Due Process: The Supreme Court has found that the Fourteenth Amendment's due process clause protects individuals from arbitrary state laws or actions that interfere with fundamental liberties. More than offering a process of fairness, courts have found that the Fourteenth Amendment prohibits states from harming an individual's ability to fully participate in society. Liberty, the Court held in *Meyer v. Nebraska*, "denotes not merely freedom from bodily restraint but also the right of the individual to contract, to engage in any of the common occupations of life, to acquire useful knowledge, to marry, establish a home and bring up children, to worship God according to the dictates of his own conscience, and generally to enjoy those privileges long recognized at common law as essential to the orderly pursuit of happiness by free men." Although the Supreme Court usually presumes that state legislation, particularly economic regulation, is valid since it is the product of a democratic process, the Court has held that substantive due process will provide some protections for parents' rights to care for their children, a woman's ability to use contraception and to have an abortion; and other significant freedoms.

Equal Protection of the Laws: Although the Declaration of Independence declared that all men were created equal, many persons living in our early republic, including Native Americans, African American slaves and women were denied fundamental rights and liberties such as the right to vote, own property and freely travel. The passage of Amendment XIV—particularly the equal protection clause—along with the power of Congress to enforce it, incorporated the Declaration's ideal into the Constitution. The equal protection clause limits the ability of states to discriminate against people based on their race, national origin, gender, or other status. For example the clause has been used to guarantee voting rights, school integration, the rights of women and minorities to equal employment opportunities and the rights of immigrants to attend public school. The extensive history of litigation under the equal protection clause in fact mirrors the struggle for civil rights of all Americans.

Apportionment and Reapportionment: Article I, Section 2 had initially provided that the number of districts in the House of Representatives would be divided among the states according to a formula in which only three-fifths of the total number of slaves in slave-owning states were counted in the state's population. Amendment XIV, Section 2 eliminated the three-fifths rule, specifically stating that representation to the House is to be divided among the states according to their respective numbers, counting all persons in each state (except Native Americans who were not taxed). The provision also punished states that did not let all males over the age of 21 vote by reducing their population for purposes of representation in Congress. With the adoption of the Nineteenth Amendment in 1920, the right to vote in federal elections was extended to women. Eighteen- to twenty-one-year-olds became voters in 1971, with the adoption of Amendment XXVI. But language in this section has been used to support the constitutionality of state laws than deny felons the right to vote.

Both Sections 3 and 4 of the Fourteenth Amendment affected persons who waged war against the Union during the Civil War and the obligations of those states who had been part of the Confederacy. Amendment XIV, Section 3 prohibits any person who had gone to war against the union or given aid and comfort to the nation's enemies from running for federal or state office, unless Congress by a two-thirds vote specifically permitted it. Amendment XIV, Section 4 allowed the federal and state governments to refuse to pay war debts of the Confederate army as well as any claims made by slave owners for their losses when slaves were freed.

Lastly, Amendment XIV, Section 5 gives Congress the power to enforce all the provisions within the whole amendment. This gives Congress the power to pass laws that protect civil rights, such as the Civil Rights Act of 1964 or the Americans with Disablilities Act of 1990.

Amendment XV

Section 1. The right of citizens of the United States to vote shall not be denied or abridged by the United States or by any State on account of race, color, or previous condition of servitude —

Section 2. The Congress shall have power to enforce this article by appropriate legislation.

What it means

The Fifteenth Amendment prohibits the use of race in determining which citizens can vote and how they do so. The last of three so-called Reconstruction Era amendments ratified in the period following the Civil War, the amendment sought to abolish one of the key vestiges of slavery and to advance the civil rights and liberties of former slaves. Section 2 of the amendment gives Congress the power to enforce it by enacting federal legislation that ensures racial equality in voting.

The ratification of the Fifteenth Amendment in 1870 had little impact for almost a century because states imposed poll taxes, literacy tests, and other restrictions that kept African Americans from voting. But the passage of the Civil Rights Act of 1964 and the Voting Rights Act of 1965, along with a number of Supreme Court decisions interpreting these laws, have done much to guarantee voting rights for African Americans and other citizens of color.

Amendment XVI

The Congress shall have power to lay and collect taxes on incomes, from whatever source derived, without apportionment among the several States, and without regard to any census or enumeration.

What it means

Article I, Section 2 and Section 9 create the "rule of apportionment," which required Congress to tax each state based on the state's population rather than taxing individuals based on personal wealth or property. For example, if the people of Delaware were four percent of the U.S. population, they would pay four percent of the total federal tax.

In 1895, in *Pollock v. Farmer's Loan & Trust Co.*, the U.S. Supreme Court declared that a federal income tax (imposed on property owned by individuals) was unconstitutional because it violated this "rule of apportionment." Although a direct income tax had previously been imposed during the Civil War, the Court's ruling in *Pollock* spurred Congress to pass and send to the states Amendment XVI. This provision gives Congress the power to impose a uniform, direct income tax without being subject to the apportionment rule. It has become the basis for all subsequent federal income tax legislation and has greatly expanded the scope of federal taxing and spending in the years since its passage. The Sixteenth Amendment was ratified by the states in 1913.

Amendment XVII

The Senate of the United States shall be composed of two Senators from each State, elected by the people thereof, for six years; and each Senator shall have one vote. The electors in each State shall have the qualifications requisite for electors of the most numerous branch of the State legislatures.

When vacancies happen in the representation of any State in the Senate, the executive authority of such State shall issue writs of election to fill such vacancies: *Provided*, That the legislature of any State may empower the executive thereof to make temporary appointments until the people fill the vacancies by election as the legislature may direct.

This amendment shall not be so construed as to affect the election or term of any Senator chosen before it becomes valid as part of the Constitution.

What it means

Popular Election of Senators: Under Article I, Section 3, two senators from each state were elected by the legislature of each state. Under this scheme senators represented the states to the federal Union, and members of the House represented the local voters in their district. But a series of scandalous elections and widespread political infighting in state legislatures, led Progressives to call for the election of senators by voters of each state. Ratified by the states in 1913, the Seventeenth Amendment provides that senators be elected by the people directly.

Amendment XVIII

[Section 1. After one year from the ratification of this article the manufacture, sale, or transportation of intoxicating liquors within, the importation thereof into, or the exportation thereof from the United States and all territory subject to the jurisdiction thereof for beverage purposes is hereby prohibited.

Section 2. The Congress and the several States shall have concurrent power to enforce this article by appropriate legislation.

Section 3. This article shall be inoperative unless it shall have been ratified as an amendment to the Constitution by the legislatures of the several States, as provided in the Constitution, within seven years from the date of the submission hereof to the States by the Congress.]

What it means

Ratified on January 16, 1919, the Eighteenth Amendment prohibited the making, transporting, and selling of alcoholic beverages. Adopted at the urging of a national temperance movement, proponents believed that the use of alcohol was reckless and destructive and that prohibition would reduce crime and corruption, solve social problems, decrease the need for welfare and prisons, and improve the health of all Americans. During prohibition, it is estimated that alcohol consumption and alcohol related deaths declined dramatically. But prohibition had other, more negative consequences. The amendment drove the lucrative alcohol business underground, giving rise to a large and pervasive black market. In addition, prohibition encouraged disrespect for the law and strengthened organized crime. Prohibition came to an end with the ratification of Amendment XXI on December 5, 1933.

Amendment XIX

The right of citizens of the United States to vote shall not be denied or abridged by the United States or by any State on account of sex.

Congress shall have power to enforce this article by appropriate legislation.

What it means

For much of American history, certain groups of people, including African Americans and women, did not have the right to vote. The struggle for women's voting rights—also known as the women's suffrage movement—lasted through much of the nineteenth and early twentieth centuries. Although some states permitted women to vote and to hold office prior to the adoption of the Nineteenth Amendment, the ratification of Amendment XIX on August 18, 1920, extended voting rights to all women. Since ratification, women's right to vote has become commonly accepted by Americans.

Amendment XX

Section 1. The terms of the President and Vice President shall end at noon on the 20th day of January, and the terms of Senators and Representatives at noon on the 3d day of January, of the years in which such terms would have ended if this article had not been ratified; and the terms of their successors shall then begin.

Section 2. The Congress shall assemble at least once in every year, and such meeting shall begin at noon on the 3d day of January, unless they shall by law appoint a different day.

Section 3. If, at the time fixed for the beginning of the term of the President, the President elect shall have died, the Vice President elect shall become President. If a President shall not have been chosen before the time fixed for the beginning of his term, or if the President elect shall have failed to qualify, then the Vice President elect shall act as President until a President shall have qualified; and the Congress may by law provide for the case wherein neither a President elect nor a Vice President elect shall have qualified, declaring who shall then act as President, or the manner in which one who is to act shall be selected, and such person shall act accordingly until a President or Vice President shall have qualified.

Section 4. The Congress may by law provide for the case of the death of any of the persons from whom the House of Representatives may choose a President whenever the right of choice shall have devolved upon them, and for the case of the death of any of the persons from whom the Senate may choose a Vice President whenever the right of choice shall have devolved upon them.

Section 5. Sections 1 and 2 shall take effect on the 15th day of October following the ratification of this article.

Section 6. This article shall be inoperative unless it shall have been ratified as an amendment to the Constitution by the legislatures of three-fourths of the several States within seven years from the date of its submission.

What it means

The four-year term of the president and vice president was fixed by the Constitution in Article II, Section 1. Because time was needed for new members to settle their affairs at home before traveling to Washington to join Congress, March 4 was initially chosen as the date both a new president and Congress would take office. However, as transportation and communications improved, this meant that the departing Congress and president would remain in office for an unnecessarily long time following the November elections. By moving the beginning of the president's new term from March 4 to January 20 (and in the case of Congress, to January 3), proponents of Amendment XX hoped to put an end to the "lame duck" syndrome (where those who were not reelected had little power to push through their policies), while at the same time allowing for a speedier transition for the new administration and legislators. The amendment was ratified on January 23, 1933.

Amendment XX also provides for succession plans if the newly elected president or vice president is unable to assume his or her position. If the president is not able to hold office, the vice president will act as president. Amendment XX gives Congress the power to pass legislation outlining a more detailed succession plan if the vice president is also not able to carry out the presidential duties until a new president and vice president are qualified.

Amendment XXI

Section 1. The eighteenth article of amendment to the Constitution of the United States is hereby repealed.

Section 2. The transportation or importation into any State, Territory, or Possession of the United States for delivery or use therein of intoxicating liquors, in violation of the laws thereof, is hereby prohibited.

Section 3. This article shall be inoperative unless it shall have been ratified as an amendment to the Constitution by conventions in the several States, as provided in the Constitution, within seven years from the date of the submission hereof to the States by the Congress.

What it means

The nation's fourteen-year experiment with prohibition ended on December 5, 1933, when Utah became the thirty-sixth state to ratify Amendment XXI. Amendment XXI returned the regulation of alcohol to the states. Each state sets its own rules for the sale and importation of alcohol, including the drinking age. Because a federal law provides federal funds to states that prohibit the sale of alcohol to minors under the age of twenty-one, all fifty states have set their drinking age there. Rules about how alcohol is sold vary greatly from state to state.

Amendment XXII

Section 1. No person shall be elected to the office of the President more than twice, and no person who has held the office of President, or acted as President, for more than two years of a term to which some other person was elected President shall be elected to the office of President more than once. But this Article shall not apply to any person holding the office of President when this Article was proposed by Congress, and shall not prevent any person who may be holding the office of President, or acting as President, during the term within which this Article becomes operative from holding the office of President or acting as President during the remainder of such term.

Section 2. This Article shall be inoperative unless it shall have been ratified as an amendment to the Constitution by the legislatures of three-fourths of the several States within seven years from the date of its submission to the States by the Congress.

What it means

Although nothing in the original Constitution limited presidential terms, the nation's first president, George Washington, declined to run for a third term, suggesting that two terms of four years were enough for any president. Washington's voluntary two-term limit became the unwritten rule for all presidents until 1940. In that year, President Franklin Delano Roosevelt, who had steered the nation through the Great Depression of the 1930s, won a third term and was elected in 1944 for a fourth term as well. Following President Roosevelt's death, in April 1945, just months into his fourth term, Republicans in Congress sought passage of Amendment XXII. FDR was the first and only president to serve more than two terms.

Passed by Congress in 1947, and ratified by the states on February 27, 1951, the Twenty-Second Amendment limits an elected president to two terms in office, a total of eight years. However, it is possible for an individual to serve up to ten years as president. The amendment specifies that if a vice president or other successor takes over for a president—who, for whatever reason, cannot fulfill the term—and serves two years or less of the former president's term, the new president may serve for two full four-year terms. If more than two years remain of the term when the successor assumes office, the new president may serve only one additional term.

Amendment XXIII

Section 1. The District constituting the seat of Government of the United States shall appoint in such manner as the Congress may direct:

A number of electors of President and Vice President equal to the whole number of Senators and Representatives in Congress to which the District would be entitled if it were a State, but in no event more than the least populous State; they shall be in addition to those appointed by the States, but they shall be considered, for the purposes of the election of President and Vice President, to be electors appointed by a State; and they shall meet in the District and perform such duties as provided by the twelfth article of amendment.

Section 2. The Congress shall have power to enforce this article by appropriate legislation.

What it means

Although New York was the nation's capital when the Constitution was ratified, the capital moved to Philadelphia in 1790 for ten years. In 1800, the District of Columbia became the official seat of government. When first established, the town had a small population of only five thousand residents. As a federal territory, however, and not a state, the inhabitants had neither a local government, nor the right to vote in federal elections. Although by 1960 the population of the District of Columbia had grown to over 760,000 people, and District residents had all the responsibilities of citizenship—they were required to pay federal taxes and could be drafted to serve in the military—citizens in thirteen states with lower populations had more voting rights than District residents.

Passed by Congress on June 17, 1960, and ratified by the states on March 29, 1961, Amendment XXIII treats the District of Columbia as if it were a state for purposes of the Electoral College, thereby giving residents of the District the right to have their votes counted in presidential elections.

Significantly, Amendment XXIII does not make Washington, D.C. a state; it merely grants its citizens the number of electors that it would have if it were a state (but no more than the smallest state). Nor does the amendment provide District residents with representation in Congress (D.C. residents have one non-voting delegate to the House of Representatives) or change the way the District is governed. Congress continues to prescribe the District's form of government.

Amendment XXIV

Section 1. The right of citizens of the United States to vote in any primary or other election for President or Vice President, for electors for President or Vice President, or for Senator or Representative in Congress, shall not be denied or abridged by the United States or any State by reason of failure to pay any poll tax or other tax.

Section 2. The Congress shall have power to enforce this article by appropriate legislation.

What it means

Although passage of the Thirteenth, Fourteenth, and Fifteenth Amendments helped remove many of the discriminatory laws left over from slavery, they did not eliminate all forms of discrimination. The Twenty-Fourth Amendment, ratified on January 23, 1964, was passed to address one particular injustice that prevented numerous citizens from voting—the poll tax, that is, a state fee on voting. Along with literacy tests and durational residency requirements, poll taxes were used to keep low-income (primarily African American) citizens from participating in elections. The Supreme Court has since struck down these discriminatory measures, opening democratic participation to all, regardless of one's ability to pay.

Amendment XXV

Section 1. In case of the removal of the President from office or of his death or resignation, the Vice President shall become President.

Section 2. Whenever there is a vacancy in the office of the Vice President, the President shall nominate a Vice President who shall take office upon confirmation by a majority vote of both Houses of Congress.

Section 3. Whenever the President transmits to the President pro tempore of the Senate and the Speaker of the House of Representatives his written declaration that he is unable to discharge the powers and duties of his office, and until he transmits to them a written declaration to the contrary, such powers and duties shall be discharged by the Vice President as Acting President.

Section 4. Whenever the Vice President and a majority of either the principal officers of the executive departments or of such other body as Congress may by law provide, transmit to the President pro tempore of the Senate and the Speaker of the House of Representatives their written declaration that the President is unable to discharge the powers and duties of his office, the Vice President shall immediately assume the powers and duties of the office as Acting President.

Thereafter, when the President transmits to the President pro tempore of the Senate and the Speaker of the House of Representatives his written declaration that no inability exists, he shall resume the powers and duties of his office unless the Vice President and a majority of either the principal officers of the executive department or of such other body as Congress may by law provide, transmit within four days to the President pro tempore of the Senate and the Speaker of the House of Representatives their written declaration that the President is unable to discharge the powers and duties of his office. Thereupon Congress shall decide the issue, assembling within forty-eight hours for that purpose if not in session. If the Congress within twenty-one days after receipt of the latter written declaration, or, if Congress is not in session, within twenty-one days after Congress is required to assemble, determines by two-thirds vote of both Houses that the President is unable to discharge the powers and duties of his office, the Vice President shall continue to discharge the same as Acting President; otherwise, the President shall resume the powers and duties of his office.

What it means

The Twenty-Fifth Amendment, ratified on February 10, 1967, clarifies what happens upon the death, removal, or resignation of the president or vice president and how the presidency is temporarily filled if the president becomes disabled and cannot fulfill his or her responsibilities. Far from being a theoretical problem, a plan of succession has frequently been necessary. On eight separate occasions, a president has died in office and one president has resigned from office. In addition, there were several occasions when the president was physically disabled and unable to meet his or her responsibilities.

For example, President Garfield was unable to govern after he was wounded by an assassin's bullet.

If a president is forced from office, dies, or resigns for any reason, the vice president becomes president. If the vice president leaves office, then the president is allowed to select a new vice president. His or her selection must be approved (confirmed) by a majority vote of both the House of Representatives and the Senate.

If the president falls seriously ill and is unable to carry out his or her duties, the president is to give notice of the disability to the president pro tempore (leader of the majority party) of the Senate and to the speaker of the House. The vice president is then authorized to step in as acting president. The president can resume office by giving notice to congressional leadership that he or she is able to do so.

If the vice president and the majority of the president's Cabinet submit to the congressional leadership a written statement that the president is not able to resume his or her responsibilities, Congress must vote on whether the president is fit to return to office. A vote of two-thirds of Congress—a so called supermajority—is required to prevent the president's return. In such a case, the vice president continues as acting president.

Amendment XXVI

Section 1. The right of citizens of the United States, who are eighteen years of age or older, to vote shall not be denied or abridged by the United States or by any State on account of age.

Section 2. The Congress shall have power to enforce this article by appropriate legislation.

What it means

Amendment XXVI gives young adults between the age of eighteen and twenty-one the right to vote. The measure is another in a line of constitutional changes that expanded the right to vote to more citizens. At the time of the ratification of the Constitution in 1788, most states limited voting to white, male citizens who were over the age of 21. It took 82 years for African American slaves to gain a constitutional right to vote, 132 years for women's suffrage and 183 years for those 18 to 21 years old to join the voting population. The impetus for this change was the passage of amendments to the Voting Rights Act in 1970 that set 18 as the minimum voting age for both federal and state elections. But when the Supreme Court ruled in *Oregon v. Mitchell* that the law applied only to federal, not state elections, Congress adopted Amendment XXVI and states quickly ratified it on July 1, 1971.

Amendment XXVII

No law, varying the compensation for the services of the Senators and Representatives, shall take effect, until an election of Representatives shall have intervened.

What it means

Amendment XXVII prevents members of Congress from granting themselves pay raises during the current session. Rather, any raises that are adopted must take effect during the next session of Congress. Proponents of the amendment believed that legislators are more likely to be cautious about increasing congressional pay if they have no personal stake in the vote. The amendment was introduced in Congress in 1789 by James Madison and sent to the states for ratification at that time. It was not until 1992 however, after public displeasure with repeated congressional pay increases, that the required three-quarters of the states ratified the measure. Unlike several other recent amendments, which contained a seven-year time limit for ratification by the states (see for example Amendments XX and XXI) Madison's proposed amendment contained no time limit for ratification.

Afterword
By David Eisenhower

Throughout the twentieth and twenty-first centuries, our nation has faced numerous challenges—economic depression, two World Wars and numerous armed conflicts, the struggle for racial justice, the nuclear arms race, the fall of communism, and most recently, terrorism at home and abroad. Yet despite these monumental obstacles, the nation has flourished—becoming the world's strongest and most prosperous nation. While the talents of the American people and the leadership of remarkable presidents has been a key to our nation's growth, beneath the dynamism and success we associate with America has been the unique system of government established by the nation's founding document, the U.S. Constitution. Whether it was a divinely "inspired" document, as many say, or merely a wise and practical arrangement, reflecting the surest insights into human nature, to direct and channel the activities of a free self-governing people, the U.S. Constitution has been the constant factor in American politics, history, and culture, the touchstone of our liberties and the key to our way of life.

There is perhaps no single feature of the Constitution that has marked its success as the blueprint of our nation. The framers of the Constitution understood that a great civilization must be governed by law and, as President Lincoln noted, guided by a government "of the people, by the people, and for the people." The framers also understood that democracy by its nature must change and that constructive change requires a reliable framework of laws, procedures, and precepts—flexible in operation and consistent in form and principle, in keeping with what Franklin Delano Roosevelt once called "essential democracy." As a framework for growth and change, the Constitution must be a "living document;" knowing that fresh Constitutional questions would constantly arise, the founders devised a role for courts and a process for ratification and amendment that was and is highly inclusive, based on discussion and debate among the citizens, not just among elite politicians and judges.

The Constitution's essential strategy is embedded in a scheme of "checks and balances" at all levels of government. At the federal level, lest any branch of government grow too powerful, the framers established three coequal branches: the presidency, the Congress, and the courts. Each of these branches has overlapping roles, which mandates cooperation in a sense, while also inviting competition and oversight among the various branches, resulting in checks or limits on the unfettered power of any of the three. Likewise, the framers of the Constitution balanced the rights of the federal union and the rights of the states, recognizing that a system with limited federal powers was both the surest way to preserve the union and the best way to gain the consent and participation of Americans in the management and direction of public affairs. The Constitution also addresses the subtlest of challenges, the protection of fundamental freedoms against what John Stuart Mill called "the tyranny of the majority." The Constitution itself, as well as the Bill of Rights and subsequent constitutional amendments, has recognized and secured the rights we all take for granted: freedom of speech; religious liberty; a justice system that presumes you are innocent until proven guilty; and rights to privacy, autonomy, equality, and due process. This broad recognition of human rights and civil liberties has assured stability at home and enabled the United States to be a champion of freedom around the world.

Indeed, Americans have a right to and do take their liberties and system of government for granted. Yet, the framers were aware that a constitutional system, no matter how well devised, could not endure without broad popular understanding and support of its essential precepts. Does that broad understanding and support of the Constitution exist, or do Americans today take too much for granted?

In particular, too few Americans, particularly young people, understand our nation's founding document, and the government and legal system it creates. A poll conducted by

Luntz Research Company for the National Constitution Center demonstrates the civics knowledge vacuum quite starkly: more of our nation's youth could name the Three Stooges than the three branches of government. Fifty-three percent of the young people surveyed knew that David Letterman prepares a nightly top-ten list, but only forty-four percent knew that the Constitution's first ten amendments are known as the Bill of Rights. Ninety-four percent of those surveyed knew that Will Smith starred in the television show Fresh Prince of Bel Air, but fewer than three percent could name William Rehnquist as the Chief Justice of the United States Supreme Court.

But constitutional illiteracy is perhaps only a symptom of a wider problem—declining civic involvement among the nation's young people. Just as their civic knowledge is limited, so also is their participation in the political process and in the civic institutions—community organizations, neighborhood associations, youth and church groups—that operate at all levels of our society. Despite the increase in youth voting during the 2004 presidential elections, voters between the ages of eighteen and twenty-four are still voting in lower numbers than they did thirty years ago. Young people today, like their parents, are less likely to read newspapers or watch television news and thus are hamstrung in their ability to participate in public policy discussions that may affect their lives. Similarly, fewer young people think that involvement in public life is important. A recent paper by Michael Delli Carpini shows that today only 19 percent of college freshman think that keeping up with public affairs is very important. In 1966, fifty-nine percent held that view.

Civic engagement is not just an abstract principle, it is essential if we wish to remain a free and prosperous nation. Whether we build a society based on religious tolerance, free from bigotry, or succumb to racial and religious hatred will not be decided by Congress or by the President, but by citizens interacting in their everyday lives. In the post–9-11 world, how society balances the need for liberty and safety will not be resolved by Justice Department officials or members of Congress alone. Our reactions as individuals when law enforcement officials ask us to take extra precautions and to surrender just a little of our privacy or liberty in order to be safe will set the parameters of the debate. President Reagan in his farewell address to the nation, reminded the American people:

> 'We the people' tell the government what to do, it doesn't tell us. 'We the people' are the driver, the government is the car. And we decide where it should go, and by what route, and how fast. Almost all the world's constitutions are documents in which governments tell the people what their privileges are. Our Constitution is a document in which 'We the people' tell the government what it is allowed to do.

But to be equipped to play this sacred role, every citizen must know and understand the ways of the government and the policy debates that will shape our future direction. To date, traditional civics education has not been able to produce demonstrably higher levels of political knowledge or understanding among high school students, nor has it been able to reverse the decline in civic involvement. According to a research study by Public Agenda conducted in 2002, thirty-seven per cent of young people found the Constitution was typically presented "in a dull and forgettable way." The study's authors present a bleak assessment: there is "ample evidence that many Americans of all ages don't understand, nor can they articulate, the Constitution's basic tenets."

This hip-pocket guide to the Constitution is one move toward reversing these trends. In one short, readable document, small enough to fit in a pocket, backpack, or purse, justicelearning.org has explained the Constitution in language that anyone can understand. My hope is that people will make it an everyday reference in the classroom, at the kitchen table, by the water cooler—wherever and whenever there is discussion of public policy issues. Look up the Second Amendment when your daughter asks you what you think of gun-control laws. Read the Twenty-sixth Amendment on your son's eighteenth birthday when he registers to vote.

Ask students to find the commerce clause, the supremacy clause, or the confrontation clause. They might enjoy the challenge; they will remember being challenged and are likely to be grateful someday when they find themselves asking the same questions we asked when putting together this book.

As a historian, I have had a unique opportunity to study the presidency. I have explored the writings and speeches of President Eisenhower and each of the presidents in the years following his tenure. I've toured the presidential libraries and listened to many of their inspiring speeches. But beyond my professional study, as the proud grandson of President Eisenhower and the son-in-law of President Nixon, I have seen presidential leadership and decision-making in action. I fully appreciate the talents and dedication of governmental figures who have made recent American history. Yet these experiences have taught me what governmental leaders in American history have always known best: that the preservation of our republic does not belong only to presidents, Supreme Court Justices, or members of Congress. It is a challenge and a responsibility that rests on all of us.

Index

Acknowledgments

Civics@Annenberg and **www.JusticeLearning.org** thanks Kathryn Kolbert, Gary Kalman, Gillian Thomas, Marsha Bolden and Eli Lesser for writing and editing the "what it means" portion of this book and gratefully acknowledge the framers of the Constitution, and the numerous historians, judges, lawyers, activists, authors, and citizens who have brought meaning to the words of our nation's founding document.

For more information about the Constitution see
www.JusticeLearning.org.

The original Constitution and the Bill of Rights are on display at the National Archives and Records Administration in Washington, D.C.

Civics@Annenberg

A project of the Annenberg Public Policy Center of the University of Pennsylvania, **Civics@Annenberg** offers high school teachers and college professors educational resources that supplement traditional curricula with relevant, hands-on lessons and materials. **Civics@Annenberg resources include the following:**

Justice Learning, a joint effort with the **New York Times Learning Network**, is a comprehensive on-line resource on civics education. The Web site offers balanced radio debates from NPR's *Justice Talking*, topical and age-appropriate articles from *The New York Times*, and a host of primary source materials, timelines, and lesson plans on a wide range of justice issues. Visit on-line at **www.JusticeLearning.org.**

Justice Talking is an award-winning public radio program hosted by NPR's Margot Adler and distributed weekly by National Public Radio. Taped before a studio audience at the National Constitution Center, the show features prominent advocates debating public policy issues of law and justice.

Student Voices is a national youth civic-engagement initiative created to address the problem of declining political participation and nonvoting by young people. The project helps high school students become informed about issues in local government and candidates in local elections. Visit on-line at **www.student-voices.org.**

The Institutions of Democracy Book Series includes both scholarly volumes and books for the public on the three branches of government, the press, and the schools. All published by Oxford University Press, these books, include Our Documents and Our Constitution.

Civics@Annenberg is made possible by the support of the Annenberg Foundation Trust at Sunnylands.